From Hilarious to Outrageous

Outrageous

An Antology of Short Stories

by Ron Rosewood

HIGHWAY 1
PUBLISHING

Published by *Highway 1 Publishing*

ISBN 978-1479235384

Printed and bound with www.createspace.com

CONTENTS

THE RUNAWAY

I was five years old, fed up with life. What a bloody disaster, nothing was going right. I wanted to damn well grow up right now, do grown up things like driving tractors, owing my own.22 rifle, going fishing every day with my own boat and motor, maybe even get ting a motorcycle with a side cart.

It would be great to own a log cabin and trap line, up in the Yukon, just like in the movie I saw at the town hall last Saturday night. That's it, trap for furs in the winter and pan for gold in the summer, now that would be really living.

Something here had to change. The key to change is to let go of fear.

I wisely waited until dad headed out into the fields, and then announced loudly to my mother. "I'm running away from home."

It was a clear warm sunny Saskatchewan morning. A perfect day to take off; after all there was no real point in running away on a cold wet miserable day. What does that get you?

"Don't forget to write us," mother paused and added, "once you learn how to write, that is." My mother was not exactly alarmed at my declaration. If dad had been there he would have straightened me out good. I'd be dragging my behind out picking stones on the summer fallow.

"Shall I make you some sandwiches?" she offered teasingly.

"What kind?" I needed to know, I don't eat just any kind of sandwich.

"How about cheese and lettuce?" She knew I liked Velveeta processed cheese, even though I often got hives after eating cheese. It was a done deal; she made my sandwich while I filled my pockets with essentials, my slingshot, my jackknife, a handful of sunflower seeds, and three carrots fresh from the garden.

Next, I went to the tool shop and got a hacksaw, ideal for falling small willows when building an overnight shelter.

Mother handed me my cheese sandwich." Good luck Ronnie." I was off. It was eight A.M., and like most runaways, I had no real plan. Down the path I headed, past our caragana hedge past the outhouse, through the grove of poplar trees along a path, towards the neighbor's house about a quarter mile away.

It was a well-worn path, as the neighbors had the first T.V in the area. Dad and I went over quite often to watch Saturday night wrestling, and boy those guys were good. My favorite was "Whipper Billy Watson." He fought fair, not like that bad guy, "Gene Kinisky"

It was a John Denver day, ideal for leaving home! The red winged blackbirds were scolding the crows trying to get at their nests. A mother mallard duck and eight ducklings were feeding in circles just off the pond's edge. Gophers were scampering from mound to mound, whistling their warnings to each other across the pasture. A red-tailed hawk circled ever so high up in the sky, ready to swoop down on unsuspecting prey.

Within ten minutes, I was over at our neighbors. Emil was out in the middle of his yard fixing the used Prefect automobile that he had recently purchased. He had seen them in England after the war. Thinking they were great, he bought one as soon as he got back to Canada.

The other men in the area drove Chevs and Fords so they chuckled at Emil's little Prefect scooting along our country dirt roads. They called him the "preacher" because student ministers drove around in small economical cars, while on their summer 'practical experience' jobs.

Emil didn't look like a preacher, as he always had a pipe between his lips, the only time I saw him without a pipe was when he was eating something, or shooting ducks with his shotgun.

He probably slept without his pipe. I never had occasion to see him sleeping.

"Hi Emil", he let me call him by his first name. He treated me like an adult. He took me along fishing, duck hunting and rabbit hunting. At the time, he had no sons only three girls, they didn't like hunting. My dad did not like to hunt or fish, he liked to work instead, so going with Emil on outings worked out fine for everyone.

"Hello Ronnie" Emil greeted me "what are you up to?"

"Nothing much, I'm just running away from home, for good, this time. I'm sick of all the work around home." It was my job to gather the eggs in the morning, bring in two arms full of firewood from the woodpile and turn the cream separator, once the milk came up from the barn twice a day.

"They keep you pretty busy alright, I won't put up with that either," he agreed with my assessment of the situation. "They're not going to miss you," he added using some reverse psychology on me, of course at the time. I knew crap about such grown up things as psychology.

This got me thinking, firstly, mom was not upset at me leaving. Now Emil does not think they are going to miss me. Hold on here a moment, am I overlooking something? Perhaps I had better rethink this "running away" idea.

I sat on that Prefect's front fender pondering my situation, watching Emil change the spark plugs and tune up the engine. He kept working without a word to me. On occasion, he would swear at the rusty bolts or warn his dog Barky to get away. Barky kept hanging around sniffing my cheese sandwich and barking his head off.

Emil could see I was deep in thought, he knew five year olds don't like to be disturbed when they're thinking. A long time went by, thirty minutes or more. I decided to eat my sandwich. Ten minutes later that was done. I jumped down off the fender. I had had a change of heart.

"Goodbye Emil" I mumbled, my shoulders hunched over, head bowed down, eyes looking at the ground, both hands in my pockets, totally ashamed of myself.

"Where are you off to Ronnie, Saskatoon or Prince Albert?" those were the nearest two cities to our farm.

"I forgot something, I have to go home." I turned to start homewards, my feet dragging reluctantly in the dirt.

"See you later." Emil said, seeing my downcast mood he added, "By the way Ronnie do you want to go fishing this evening? The Fish and Game Department just opened Shannon Lake, it was stocked three years ago. The talk is there are large pickerel in there now." He kindly offered up a solution to my self-inflicted dilemma.

"That would be great! I answered. I'll go home and check my fishing rod and reel, see you later." Off I went, bouncing and smiling, happy as a clam. Life was suddenly beautiful.

Arriving home, I sat on the swing and ate a carrot. I thought to myself, "Dad would be happier if he took time out to sit on a swing and eat a carrot. I must tell him that when he comes home tonight."

"Oh it's you Ronnie, home already? "Mother was going by with a basket full of laundry to hang on the clothesline. She did not seem surprised to see me, even though I had only been gone two hours. "I thought we wouldn't see you for at least three years." Her eyes sparkled, amused with my antics.

"Emil is taking me fishing, to Shannon Lake, later today, I can always run away tomorrow, after all there is no hurry."

"No, no hurry at all, dear."

Mothers knew how to make a fellow seem important even when he was wrong.

LES & DENNY CELEBRATE THE NEW YEAR

Les and Denny were getting ready to celebrate New Year's Eve. In fact, they were just finishing celebrating last New Years.

Cracking open another beer, Denny handed it to Les, getting another for himself from the fridge, and taking a man-sized swig. He turned to Les. "Happy New Year, Les," Denny said raising his beer.

"Which one?" was Les' garbled reply, hesitating to lift his bottle.

"Which one what?" Denny didn't like trick questions.

"Which year did you mean 2011 or 2012?" fired back Les. "You wished me a happy new year Denny boy. I need to know which blinking year you're referring to."

Denny was not one to take embarrassment lightly. "Les, what kind of a stupid question is that? How the hell should I know which year? How about 1492? Was that a good year for you?

"Look Denny, don't be an idiot. If you wish somebody a Happy New Year, you should be able to state exactly which year you mean." Les took a long drink.

"Am I supposed to read your damn mind Les?" Denny reasoned. "How do I know if you had a happy 2011, and even more unknown to me, is if you are going to have a happy 2012? Now you tell me which one it should be."

"Denny, for goodness sake look around. We have sat here for the last 365 days drinking. Shouldn't that give you a clue whether I had a happy year or not?" Les had it half right.

Denny filled in the other half. "Look Les you may look happy drinking beer after beer after beer. In fact, you may have been so happy that you forgot if you were happy or not. How can I tell if you were happy or happy sad? Come to think of it, do you even know what happy is any more?"

"Sure I know what happy is." Les was bluffing. Denny had him confused.

Denny tried again. "O.K. then Les, if you know what happy is, then simply tell me to what degree you are happy. Then we will decide which year to apply my saying 'happy new year 'to. If you were overwhelmingly happy in 2011 then we will agree that 2011 is the year for which I wished you a happy new year. If you were under whelming happy, then we will say I am wishing you a happy new year for a better year in 2012. How does that sound?"

"Denny, let me get this straight. I have to decide if I was happier in 2011 than I might be in 2012?" Les used his logic again. "But Denny 2012 hasn't started yet. What if I say 2011, and then it turns out that 2012 is much better than 2011? Would I not be making a big mistake? I don't want to do that. That goes against everything I stand for."

Denny had enough. "Yeah, Yeah, don't use that moral argument on me. I know exactly what you stand for Les. It's referred to as B.S., in polite social circles."

Les ignored the insult. He had another question. "Besides Denny what kind of scale do I use to measure my happiness index?"

"Use a scale of 1 to 10.That's all there is to it Les. Pick a blinking number. If it is more than five, we choose 2011. If it is, fewer than 5 then we choose 2012. Tell me which number works the best for you." He stared at Les and added. "Now, pick a number Les."

Les replied, "I pick number 5."

"You can't pick 5, 5 is a tie between the two years. It does not solve the problem. Did we not agree that you would pick a number either over 5 or fewer than 5 now choose again?"

Les replied, "I agreed to nothing, I chose 5. That's my number. I want number 5."

Denny got an exasperated look on his face. "Look Les, I made a mistake by trying to wish you a happy new year. *I take back my happy new year.*"

Les looked hurt "What do you mean you take it back? Are you saying you don't want to wish me, your best friend, a happy new year? Besides you can't take it back any more than you can take back a ball that you've already thrown?"

Denny shook his head in bewilderment. "This is not a ball game Les. There are no happy New Year wishes for you, because I took them back."

"What kind of a friend are you if you can't wish me a happy new year?" Les demanded to know, slamming his bottle on the coffee table top. "We've been wishing each other a happy new year for 35 years."

Denny relented, seeing that he had angered Les. "Happy New Year Les, I wish you all the best."

Les drank some more. "Which year do you mean Denny?"

Denny raised his voice. "I mean 2011 Les, because 2012 will not be a good year for you."

"Why not?" Les barked back. "How do you know?"

Because, Les, at midnight which is in ten minutes from now, I will shoot you!"

"Now why didn't you just say that in the first place?" Les raised his beer bottle. "Happy New Year Denny."

THE BIGGER THE LIE

The town of Maple Springs was rippling with the latest news. A group of business developers was to address town council that night with a proposal that was to bring new industry to town. The project would create 80 new jobs, with prospects for many more in the future.

A "News Leak" to the Springs Recorder showed a company, by the name A.R. Development Corporation from Toronto, had preliminary discussions with the town's business development officer, Harry Cohen, relating to local and government funding for the project.

It was further reported there would be opportunities for local residents to participate in the lucrative venture by way of a trust unit offerings. Positions at all levels were to be predominately filled by locals. The meeting was to be at 8 P.M. Thursday evening. Everyone was welcome.

Les and Denny, driving home from the Wednesday night harness races, heard the report on the CKQM radio news. Les was interested. "How about it Denny, shall we go?"

"Sounds like a scam to me Les."

"The town council is party to it. Surely they can't be in on a scam?"

"All right, I guess attending the meeting can't do any harm, pick me up at 7.30."

The attendance was beyond expectations. Cars were parking on the front lawn of the town hall property. People were lining up to receive a brochure as they entered the hall. Les and Denny took theirs' and seated themselves on the last remaining bench.

"Boy what a huge turn out!" exclaimed Les.

"Just hold your water Les; let's wait for the man's presentation." The crowd wasn't impressing Denny. Glancing at the brochure increased his skepticism, it stated. "This proposal is to raise Angora rabbits, create a wool processing plant and a rabbit meat processing facility."

Denny commented, "What kind of hair raising idea is this?" They both laughed at the unintended pun.

The meeting began with the mayor Duncan McKenzie in the chair.

"Ladies and gentlemen, now I will turn the floor over to Mr. Art Burns of A.R. Development Corporation for his presentation."

Art Burns stepped up, very business like, dressed to the hilt in his Italian double breasted gray suit and red tie." Thank you Mr. Mayor. I will begin by saying that this is the fifth project of this type that I have spearheaded in the past three years." Flashing a confident smile at the crowd, he continued.

"I am proud to report that all the ventures are successful, thriving and expanding. The demand for our products escalates each month. The crowd is humming excitedly. Art was pushing all the right buttons, the audience was gasping in unison wanting to hear more.

He added. "The reason we have been so successful is that this is an integrated project. We build the barns and plant buildings using local materials and workers. The rabbits are bred here.The food pellets are made here.The wool is processed here, and the rabbit meat plant is right here. To top all this off we can bag and sell rabbit dropping for extra income. This form of fertilizer is extremely popular with strawberry growers because of its high nitrogen content. This large-scale project gives us a tremendous cost advantage over the smaller family run operations in the industry. Our investors have seen annual returns of well over 15% per year six months after the initial start up and upwards of 20%.in years 2 and 3."

The crowd was unable to contain itself any longer, their clapping, escalates into a dull roar.

"Furthermore with the help of your business development officer Mr. Cohen, we have applications with the federal government business incentive program for grants amounting up to 3.5 million dollars. The only requirement left, before approval, is that, the participating community has to raise a matching amount. Once done this will give us a total of 7 million dollars of seed capital."

"Now I will open the floor up to questions from the floor. Please proceed to the microphone at the center of the hall to ask your questions." A dozen people rushed to the area, the first was the local school principal Don Miller, the highest paid man in town. He was looking for a place to spend the savings accumulated from his huge salary.

"What are your projected annual sales six months after start up?"

"Wool products are estimated at one million dollars and meat sales at six hundred thousand dollars the first year; three million in wool and two million in meat for the second year."

"That sounds exaggerated. How can you achieve such fast results?"

"Remember sir, we are talking rabbits here. A doe starts breeding at 16 weeks, has a gestation period of 31 days. Over a useful life of 18 months, she has 10-12 litters of 6-8 surviving rabbits. That folks adds up to 77 rabbits per doe. Those rabbits start producing after 16 weeks. If you do the math, a single doe can be responsible for the birth of 1548 rabbits in her useful lifetime. Multiply that by 5000 does and times it by 66.65%. That my friends amounts to 5,158,710 rabbits per year by the end of year two."

The enormity of the numbers stuns the crowd. They can almost feel the wallets in their pants bulging with newfound profits.

Another question comes from the floor. "Reports say this will create 80 full time jobs. How much will your wage rates be?"

"Hourly pay rates will range from $ 10 for line workers to $ 15 for shift supervisors, again remember folks, these are permanent full time positions." The crowd nods approval those are fair rates for 1976.

"How do we make an investment?" asks Mr. Small a retired chicken farmer.

"The investment trust units are $ 2,500 each. You can buy up to 20 units. We set a maximum of 20 units so everyone can participate. We will be leaving no one out."

"Put me down for the max, I'm in." Mr. Small replied, reaching for his wallet.

"In a few minutes, I will be at the back of the hall, at the desk set up there. I also have three assistants to help explain the procedures and begin taking applications. Cheques are acceptable and we will be mailing you your trust certificates within 30 days."

"If there are no further questions, we will proceed to the sign-up desk. I wish to thank your town council and officers in assisting us with our project. We made a deposit on the Kooster property, of 50 acres this morning, as the site for our plant."

People began lining up ten deep, in three rows. Within 2 hours, the entire units were fully subscribed. The financing was a major success. Les was one of the first to sign up and pay for his allotment of 10 units, totaling twenty five thousand dollars.

"Les, don't you think you should be checking with Stella before signing up?" Denny suggested.

"You saw the rush, there wasn't time." They drove homeward, Les dropped Denny off. Denny, had stayed out of the frenzy, electing not to invest

Stella was waiting on the porch, as Les drove up. She had been listening to the radio about the events at the town hall meeting, knowing Les was inclined to gamble on just this type of thing.

"Les, come here, now. Look, I hope you weren't foolish enough to invest in that rabbit-shit business, where you?"

"I couldn't help it 15% is a lot better than the 5% we are getting from the bank."

"Les, tell me, tell me right now how much did you invest? Don't try lying to me."

"I bought 10 units."

"Damn you, stop fudging Les, how much money did you spend?"

"Only twenty five thousand. Angel." Les began stepping back.

"Don't you Angel me Les! That money was to pay off our mortgage. Why did you do it?"

"They are paying 15%, our mortgage is only 7% ,we are ahead by 8% this way."

"That was a joint account Les. Tomorrow you and I are going down to the bank and stopping payment on that cheque. Do you hear me?"

"Yes Angel."

"Come to bed now. We'll talk more in the morning."

"Yes Angel." Les was happy he had Stella looking after him. 'Today will be yesterday, tomorrow.' he thought, following her up the stairs.

Thirty days later the option on the property expired. No one had gotten his or her investment certificates. Harry Cohen the town's business development officer had to resign. The mayor Duncan McKenzie lost his seat in the fall election. The 350 investors were out 3.5 million dollars. Art Burns of Toronto could not be located by the police. It had all been a swindle. It was a sad time in Maple Springs.

If you are traveling through town, any time soon, never, never mention the Angora Rabbit Project.

CHRISTMAS EVE 1949

As an eight year old the wonders of a Christmas Eve in north central Saskatchewan was a memorable day.

The routine was the same. A gathering of the clan at our grandparents' place, and clan it was. In addition to the grandparents, there were their 5 adult children with their spouses as well as 14 grand children, a total of 26.

Everyone lived within a five-mile radius, on individual small farms, so distance was not a factor.

The main threat was the winter weather and in those early years, cars were parked in the garage from November 15 to April15. We used covered sleighs pulled by draft horses were the only mode of winter transportation.

On December 24 at 4 pm dad would hitch King and Queen, not exactly original horse names, to the caboose that was in effect a cab-like structure on sleigh runners. The cab was cozy with a small wood heater. It had a tin chimney, from which drifted a smoke plume as the horses dragged the contraption along at four miles per hour.

It was your basic outhouse on runners, not as tall as an outhouse and no holes in the seats, but it did have windows for peering out into the starlit landscape.

The frozen snow was crunching under our boots as we made our way from the house to the caboose. Dad's blue cigarette smoke would permeate the caboose air, as we rode along. We were used to it, perhaps even enjoying the secondhand smoke. The little wood burning heater kept us warm in addition to our parkas, mitts and rubber overshoes. We thought we were the luckiest people in the world. We defied anyone to tell us different.

In an hour, we arrived at the inviting little valley where Grandfather homesteaded and lived for some 60 years. He chose a less productive quarter section for a home site preferring the low treed hills with a ravine valley. It reminded his of his Hungarian homeland.

We kids loved it as it differed from our flatland farms. It was magical; there was always something to do. We went, tobogganing in winter, berry picking in summer, gathered wild hazel nuts in fall hunting was terrific with partridge n the willows and scores of ducks and wild geese in the marsh adjacent to the farm.

Soon all 26 of us were jamming into an 800 square foot cedar clad house. The dinner was preceded with a rather lengthy grace, in fact a mini sermon. Grandfather took every opportunity to ram home how we should be so ever grateful for everything we had received in the past, in the present and for the coming years. However, I thought at the time, the appeal of candy and nuts prevailed over eternal salvation. I did not tell anyone of my thoughts or I would have spent the rest of the evening, alone, in the cold caboose, in the dark

With the conclusion of the "sermon on the snow bank", we dug into the fried chicken, cabbage rolls, mashed potatoes, veggies. We finished by eating fruitcake filled with green and red cherry pieces. Nuts and candies were available for those that still needed more.

After our meal, there was more Christmas Carol singing, in Hungarian of course, with the theme being the birth of the Little One. To confirm the event we looked at slides in a new-fangled view master and by golly, there was the Little Fellow, in the manger. The three wise men praying away, their camels parked behind the stable. The North Star was blazing down on the whole scene. There was no disputing the wonder of it all. We all wished we could have been there in person.

After about another hour of interacting with cousins, aunts and uncles, we bundled up and retraced our steps homeward. King and Queen, after standing around for five hours in their harnesses, gladly pulled us home in the clear cold winter moonlight.

Once home we were rewarded with a single gift each. Mine was a pair of 5 ' spruce, cross-country skis, $2 in the Sears catalog. It was, a present that give me many hours of enjoyment for several years.

Yes, Christmas Eve 1949, was a memorable day.

LES GETS A NEW LAPTOP

"Dammit Les groaned as his computer crashed and burned. "Where will I get $3000 for another?" He was recently retired, getting by on two small pensions. There was no wiggle room in his budget.

His friend, Dennis Inkman, arrived for their weekly drinking session. Hearing of Les' dilemma, he offered a solution. "Buy the damn computer on credit, like everybody else."

"That's not my style."

"Style? Now you got style?" Denny cracked open the beer.

"I need cash. "Lee took a beer.

"How?"

"Denny, that's what I'm asking you."

"Dennis was clever; he had it "I've got it, get money first, then a computer."

"Denny boy, from whom do I get the money?"

"Easy, join a computer dating service, meet a partner, she gives you the money."

"I don't have a computer, remember?"

"The library has."

"I can't hang around down there for hours."

"You don't have to. Just register your profile. Make sure you mention that you're 6 feet tall, a professional, and you like operas."

"I'm 5'10" a truck driver, I hate operas".

"Do you want a new computer?"

"O.K., O.K., I'm a six foot tall, opera loving professional, then what?"

"Two days later 20 eager women will want to meet you. Take them for coffee."

"All at the same time?"

"No dummy, one at a time. Now tell me how many cups of coffee can you drink in a day?"

"Ten, I guess."

"There, it will take you 2 days."

"When do I get my computer money?"

"After your search is down to the right woman."

"How?"

"Easy, half the women will not like you.at all."

"How can I tell?"

"They will be smiling, but their eyes will be closed."

"O.K., that leaves ten."

"Of those half will have money. The other half wants money. Tell all 10 you have no money. Five more finish with you right there. Now you have five with money. One will give it to you money."

"Which one? How do I ask?"

"Tell each one you have a sick mother in Toronto. You need $3000 to go see her."

"Will they believe that?"

"One probably will."

"Which one?"

"The one that lost a parent suddenly and did not get to see him or her."

"How will I know?"

"She will be crying as she reaches for her cheque book."

"Then I can buy my computer?"

"Yes, but you have to stay at my place for a week first. Remember, you'll be in Toronto visiting your sick mother."

"When you get back and she sees my new computer, she will ask where I got it."

"Tell her your mother recovered and she surprised you with a parting gift.'"

"You're a good friend Denny Inkman. You think of everything."

"Les old buddy. I'll drink to that."

PRAIRIE TASTES

January – it's six a.m. the blizzard has finally blown itself out. We open the door to find a two foot drift of snow against the door. Trudging to the log barn we hear the cows mooing in unison, waiting for their oats and half gallon of crushed oats in exchange for a gallon of warm milk. The cats sit near meowing to us to squirt some milk their way.

February. It is still snowing. After the morning chores we have our oatmeal with cream, sugar, and cinnamon. It's Sunday, we are off to visit our grandparents. They live in an area with hills. We take our skiis, and toboggans scrubbed with honeycomb wax. Holding our breath we tackle a steep hill. For added excitement it has a tree foot drop at the bottom. We go flying through the fog trying to stay upright. Some of us manage, others fall on their behinds.

March – the first signs of spring, as light purple crocuses push aside the last melting layer of snow. We plant seeds of tomatoes, radishes and lettuce in tobacco can containers filled with sod. After thee weeks the little plants are transferred to the cold frame on the sunny side of the house. Flocks of wild Mallards and Canada geese quack and honk as they wing their way north.

April. The crows are back, gathering noisily in the woodlot beginning to occupy last year's nests or constructing new ones. The fields are drying out in the warm spring sun. Dad is repairing machinery anticipating planting wheat, barley and oats.

May – the ice is off the sloughs, the planting is being finished. We paint the boat in anticipation of getting out on the lakes for some early pickerel. The school kids are practicing their high jumping, running, and softball skills, preparing for the field day trials in our nearest town. Radishes, lettuce and green onion shoots supplement out meat and potatoes fare.

June – hooray school is winding down, teacher hollers, scolds and threatens us daily. The wheat crops have sprung to life like green carpeting on the fields. The fishing in the, windless evenings is spectacular. Fresh creamed pea soup is served up three times a week, followed by jelly rolls filled with strawberry jam. We go crazy waiting, ,as mother serves up cream fresh pea soup with jelly roll.

July – we are busy haying in the meadows and having it baled into 80 pound bales We start collecting them in a hay wagon pulled by a tractor. It's hard work, however we get the knack of using leverage with the bale strings and hoist bales eight feet into the air. We like picking Saskatoon berries, of course we eat our share, as we pick, what we don't eat mother makes into fruit, or pies.

August – there is a lull in activities as the crops fill out, we have to spray the fields to keep the bugs in check. The weekend ball tournaments are on, rotating from town to town. We watch, while munching on hot dogs liberally covered with mustard and drink a cream soda as a chaser. We talk to people we haven't seen since last year's tournament and promise to visit each other more often, we never do. School starts, the teacher is happily scolding us for not remembering the math formulas, who cares.

September – harvesting begins, hampered by fall rains, the smell of freshly cut stubble fills the air as wheat streams from the combine hopper into the truck. Duck hunting season opens, we love shooting ducks. We hate eating them, they are tough and gamey, tainted with fish and frogs flavors. Corn on the cob is ready, if an early frost didn't wipe out the whole crop. It's time to put the snow tires on the vehicles.

October – my favorite time, we gather up the potatoes, carrots, cabbage heads and other garden goodies. We look for the perfect pumpkin amongst the pumpkin patch. Of course in Saskatchewan any pumpkin larger that a softball is considered a winner. One as large as a soccer ball is classed as a miracle. People talk for weeks about their prowess as growers. Others use the flimsy excuse that they were too busy growing real crops instead of growing giant pumpkins

November – Everything freezes up solid. We go skating on the sloughs, trying to race the muskrats swimming under the ice beneath out feet. We clink up the spaces between the logs in the barn and haul logs in from the woodlot. We saw and split the logs into firewood lengths for our space heaters.

December – the snow is back, the easy life is over. We haul ice blocks from the sloughs to melt for wash water. We skate when the sun is out and we get ready for Christmas by putting in our request for ten gifts. We are happy for the one gift we get.

The year is a success.

CONFIRMING MY REINCARNATION

Let me tell you right at the outset, I am not a religious person. I don't marvel at the height and beauty of our churches. I do not watch the sky for bolts of flashing lightening coming my way. Do I see burning bushes? Yes, every summer on the nightly news, California must be the most sacred place on earth.

Neither do I think we evolved from trash left behind by alien visitors, as some prominent scientists have theorized. No, I think the answer lies somewhere between the two extremes, hence my growing interest in reincarnation.

Reincarnation principles, as I gather from my library browsing's are based on the premise that I have been here before, I are here now, and I will be returning back again and again. That sounds like my kind of pudding. The reason for this coming back requirement is that I have not fulfilled my goal of being an exceptionally good person. For that reason I am ordered back to get it right.

What are the odds of me being a good person? Hitting a hole in one in golf has odds of 12,700 to 1. If those odds hold true for reincarnation, I am destined to be reincarnated numerous times. Hell, I may make it into the Guinness book, before I'm through!

Now this is the confusing part. I come back without instructions. I'm not told where I goofed up last time, or the time before that. Can you visualize that! Now unexpectedly, I am supposed to excel at goodness and civility. What am I to do? It is a seventy-year long road trip without a map, getting lost and failing is a certainty!

Being a nonconformist is my nature. I am not a half-blind sheep that follows goats around. I make my own way. I am not a bad person, even if I do bad things occasionally. What about the good things, don't they count? My way of thinking is if I do a bad thing and a good thing then I'm still even, one balances out the other. Here is what happened to me.

I was three days short of thirteen. It was summer. My parents took me to my aunt and uncle's farm for a week, "to give you a little holiday" they said. I suspected they wanted me out of their way so they could enjoy some peace and quiet.

I was mad, "We live on a farm for goodness sake!" I shot back, 'what kind of holiday is being on another farm ?"

I had my heart set on camp Wakonda, where I saw city kids swimming, canoeing, and having a hell of a good time chasing the camp girls in the adjoining buildings. I was annoyed as hell. "Dad do something." I pleaded. Dad's motto was, a man has to do what a man has to do. He had gleaned this from reading western adventures of "The Cimmeron Kid." Today the Cimmeron Kid was rather silent

My older sister was in the back seat with me. "The Hoarder," as she was fondly known, was chewing away on candy she had saved since Christmas. "See what I have," she said, sneering and teasing.

"Give me some of that damned candy, right now!" I shouted at her. I lived for the moment, my candy had been eaten by New Year.

"Look you miserable control freak, give me some or I will tell Mom.

Mom of course was right there in the front seat and heard it all. She was already reaching for the fly swatter resting on the dashboard, it was her favorite attack weapon. "Do you want m e to get after you two?" she threatened. Surely it was a rhetorical question, who in there right mind wanted a few well placed swats across the side if their face.

22

I got some candy.

Dad seemed unaware of the ruckus, perhaps he chose to ignore it. He knew his place, in fact in their courtship days, mother had taken the lead and demanded he marry her or 'buzz off," as he had wasted three years of her life on him up to that point. It was not the classic heart filled proposal like you see at the movies. Dad was on his knees in record time and the wedding day was set.

Arriving at our destination, I was shoved out of the car and given a quick goodbye. "Have a nice time Ronnie," smiled my mother, "we'll pick you up in a week."

I stood there in the dusty driveway, the summer sun beating down, dust swirls blew toward the yard from the fields. I had on my brown braided rim, cowboy hat, my Roy Rodgers twin cap gun set in their red leather holster. I held my BB gun in my right hand and a shopping bag of extra clothes in my left hand. Tears crept down from under my $12 pair of clear frame glasses. Feeling abandoned and unappreciated, I watched my parents speeding out of sight, my sister still sneering and waving her bag of candy through the back window.

My aunt prompted me to action. 'Come in and have some cherry Kool-Aid'

"Thanks Aunt Margaret." I whimpered, as I heavy heartedly made my way to the kitchen table. *Some holiday this was going to be*, I thought as I downed two large glasses of the drink.

For the first two days, I wandered around the farm snaring a few stupid gophers and killing a dozen worthless sparrows with my BB gun. All that action made a hungry boy out of me. My aunt had gone to town and my uncle was out spraying the hell out of the weeds in the fields. I began snooping in the pantry for some goodies. Nosing around I saw a package of ice cream cones on the top shelf; just the thing for a little snack. There were eight, I had two, then two more. Well you know the rest of the story. I ate them all. I threw the packaging into the wood burning cook stove.

Now that was bad, right? Well, yes, it could be considered bad, not the burning of the package. I mean stealing and eating the cones without permission. I felt justified because there was tacit permission there in the fact that they were left out in plain view in an unlocked pantry. I not only felt entitled, but justified as well.

In about an hour aunt Margaret returned. "I have a surprise for the birthday boy!" she exclaimed. It was a hell of a surprise all right, as she displayed a carton of strawberry ice cream. It was my favorite kind.

Boy oh boy, I thought, how is this afternoon going to play out? Ice cream needs cones, and I had eaten all the cones.

Aunt Margaret disappeared into the pantry and began rummaging around amongst the jars of preservatives. "I was sure I had some cones in here." She backed out of the pantry and looked at me. "I wonder what happened to them. Is my mind playing tricks on me?"

"I have heard of that happening." I replied, trying to reinforce that thought. "Grandpa forgets lots of stuff all the time."

"Ronnie have you seen them?" She stood there glaring at me, she pursed her lips so hard I thought she might dislodge her fillings. She was through speculating, she was now into the investigating phase of the missing cones.

Staring at her and shaking my head negatively, I considered my options. I could say I had eaten them by mistake. That was a lame excuse. My other choice was to remain silent and act dumb. I chose to clam up.

Aunt Margaret was not done with me yet. I was her prime suspect and the only one. "Maybe I should call your mother to come and get you." She was steamed. As she glared at me I could not raise my eyes higher than her ample bosom, the longer I looked the larger her bust seemed to get. It was a short-lived diversion. I had to come up with something. I did not want Mom and her fly swatter involved. This did not look good.

The day was saved when my uncle Steve came in from the fields. "Hi Ronnie, are you behaving?" He knew I was a brat and he was usually amused at my antics.

"Hi Uncle," I took the opportunity to speak first. "The ice cream cones are missing. Have you seen them?" He noticed the sly smile crossing my face. He had guessed what had happened.

"Maybe Brownie ate them." he suggested, referring to the family dog. He turned and headed for the bathroom.

After my uncle washed up, the party started. "Lawrence" a neighbor kid came over with his mother. Don't make the mistake of calling him "Larry." No his name was Lawrence and there he stood attired in a white shirt, black tie, black pants and black sport coat. He was your typical Sunday School graduate. He was a Mamma's boy, if there ever was one, *yes please this and yes please that*, it was enough to make me barf. I couldn't stand the little bastard, what a suck up!

There he was, there I was, I decided to put up with him for the afternoon. I could invite him out to the gopher field tomorrow and clean his clock out there. To ensure he would come, I would tell him I saw some religious sign in the mud along the slough that looked like Jesus. He would go nuts over something like that! Yes, he was mine for sure.

The party started. Uncle Steve played his guitar. Brownie the border collie howled along to the tunes as uncle played 'Home on The Range' and 'You are my Sunshine'. We dunked for apples, pinned the tail on the donkey and played darts. I was the center of attention and had the most fun. Hot dogs and potato salad followed and then Ice cream and cake. My Aunt give me a scolding glance as she served out the ice cream in bowls.

Now fifty-seven years later and I might add there have been many more questionable deeds perpetrated by me, some much more serious than the missing cone affair. I now have a dilemma. Am I destined to be reincarnated again and returned to earth? What does it take to succeed? Perhaps Lawrence who went on and became a prominent and well-respected clergyman could tell me. He would have the answers; however, he died suddenly last spring before I could visit him. Maybe the bastard will send me some sort of sign or message from wherever he is.

I am in the sunset of my life, no doubt, accounts will have to be balanced, not in my favor, I fear. Am I destined to come back for yet another go around? Pass the strawberry ice cream please.

THE FALLING OUT

Les and Denny, drinking buddies for thirty years, weren't speaking. What prompted this?

Here is what happened. Last Saturday morning, Les was at Safeway feeling melons. He rarely bought any. Melons don't go with beer. However holding a softball sized melon in the palm of each hand invigorated him. Les stood there invigorating and daydreaming, when an ash blond woman strolled up. She stopped and smiled "Hi there cowboy, how do they feel? "She giggled. "I'm Mandy, what's your name?"

"Les, Les, Les Brown" he stuttered. Embarrassed, he studied the little blond bombshell. Les was a confirmed bachelor, or so he thought. Women interfered with a man's God-given right to drink, smoke and gamble. Women wanted men to work hard, pay the mortgage, pay the bills, make the car payments, and spring for expensive holidays. All that seemed trivial now. He was smitten. He put the melons down. It was time to leave the world of make believe and walk the tight rope of love.

Well they spent the weekend together, frolicking like kids in a sandbox. Everything was fun and games. On Monday morning they agreed to meet again on Friday; when Les returned from truck driving.

On Monday night Denny, a warehouse supervisor, attended a night school class to upgrade his first aid skills. Guess who was giving the course on mouth to mouth recitation? You're right, it was Mandy. After two hours of learning mouth to mouth, Denny was a slow learner, he suggested that they go for coffee.

She readily agreed that coffee would be nice. After two hours of drinking lattes they became inseparable.

Les arrived home on Friday and phoned Denny saying they could not meet at the Fraser Arms sports bar. Denny was cool with that.

Les phoned Mandy leaving a message on her answering machine. He showered, bought flowers and wine and drove over to her apartment.

Since Denny was now free, he decided he would surprise Mandy. He got some wine and Chinese food and hurried over to Mandy's apartment.

They nearly crashed their cars in Mandy's parking lot.

Les exited his car. "Denny, are you lost"

"I'm here to see my new girl, Mandy, I park in space 33."

"Your new girl" Les barked "I arranged this date a week ago!"

"We had coffee on Monday night." Denny sneered.

Les reminded him. "Denny, ten bucks worth of coffee, is just that, ten bucks worth of coffee?"

"Well, we'll go up to her apartment and straighten this out!" Exclaimed Denny.

As they entered the apartment building, Mandy strolled out of the elevator, arm in arm with the local radio announcer Andy Flowers. (His real name was Andy Sivinsky)

Les and Denny looked at Mandy. She looked at them; they had nothing to say to one another.

Les relented, "Denny boy, I'll trade these roses for half of your Chinese food."

"You're on, Buddy."

HERO OF THE DAY

The year was 2292. Earth was losing its' ability to sustain life.

Roger, 42, was considered old. Not that life expectancy had dropped from the early 2000's figure of 78. No not that, but rather due to new international laws passed in the year 2202

The "43 plus one law" as it was called, mandated that every person regardless of race, color or status was euthanized at age 43, no exceptions. The reason for the law was evident; the world powers could not control births. Therefore, they controlled who lived, or more precisely who did not live.

The figure of 43 was arrived at by assessing a person's usefulness to society, as a working person. It considered the cost of health care for over 40 year Old's and also obligations to children who would be grown up by the time parents attained 43. Everyone had to bite the proverbial 'bullet' and have his or her life end one day after his or her 43rd birth date. The reason for the one-day grace was also clear; no one wished to die before his or her 43rd birthday party.

Each day a lovely website list appeared on the internet called "Heroes of The Day." It showed the names of all good world citizens who complied with the 43 plus 1 law. Indexed by country, city and street, it was easy to determine from where each hero originated.

Roger was downing his fifth rum and coke drink. The seriousness of the moment finally sank in. By noon tomorrow, he would be incinerator fire, smoke and ash.

This give a new meaning to the phrase of "High Noon," a hold over from the Gary Cooper 1952 movie title. Cooper with courage and straight shooting extradited himself from his situation.

Roger was not accorded such an opportunity nor did he have the necessary skills to save himself. Or did he?

He stood in his back yard garden party on a beautiful mid summer day gazing out over the blue Pacific ocean. While listening to the lively band music, with his wife Norma age 38 and his kids Jason age 20 and daughter Christine age 18 his mind raced to find a solution to his dilemma. Live or die. It was that simple, yet it was that complicated.

He felt embarrassed and also ashamed. Did not his brother Rodney make the ultimate sacrifice just two years ago? Also, several cousins and friends obeyed the new law. He had been indoctrinated into the belief of serving the greater good, as the "Law" required. Yet he harbored the desire to circumvent the law to save himself. Selfish? Yes, most would call it that. Smart? That too. Roger was a selfish, smart person. He could live with that.

It was now nine p.m. The party guests knew the routine. One by one, they quietly took off their party hats, put down their drinks, stopped joking around, gathered up their belongings and became somber. They dutifully came up to Roger, standing at the side gate, and wished him a final goodbye.

They had done this before. In fact most people attended at least one "final" birthday every month, some times two and in a few cases final parties for twins. It was their sworn duty and they obliged, knowing all too well their turn was coming. Few words were spoken; few tears were shed, after all the law was the law. It was necessary to provide space for the children and for grand children. Rare because most people did not live long enough to see their grand children. This was reality in the 23rd century. The law had worked for 90 years, Roger nor anyone else, could do squat about it. Or could they?

After doing, a cleanup of the party trash and stacking the rented lawn furniture, Roger and Norma retired to the living room. Roger smiled at the thought of the words 'Living room'. *'Not much' longer he thought,* as they turned on the 10 o'clock nightly news. The news was predictable, as usual, flooding in China, an earthquake in Indonesia and 2 more countries fighting in Africa.

There was no longer any news of cancer, diabetes, heart disease, or aids. All the research labs had been closed down. There was no need to unduly prolonging anyone's life. The world was using natural diseases and disasters, as yet another way of curbing population growth.

Then an interesting news item caught Rogers' attention. An international space mission was blasting off for Mars tomorrow. That in its self was not unusual, as there had been twice yearly flights to Mars for the better part of 90 years now. They were billed as tourist flights and were rather costly, two million dollars a person. Because of the rates, only wealthy, influential people took the flights, passenger lists were not made public.

Suddenly a thought struck Roger. Where these flights a way of some rich people circumventing the 43 plus 1 law?

Roger went to his computer and began to compare the names of prominent people on the 43 plus 1 list with news articles some 20 years back that referred to celebrities' ages. Within two hours, he had a list of over 62 persons that should have been scooped up under the 43 plus 1 law but were not on the "Hero of The Day" list. Could they have been secreted away to Mars or some other space destination to enjoy a normal retirement life?

"Those dirty bastards are using this law and earth's resources to finance their own escape routes to another world. The bigger the lie, the more likely they think we will believe it." Roger exclaimed.

He picked up the phone and called his congressional representative. After 22 minutes on the phone, he turned to Norma. "Honey, go pack we are leaving earth one hour before noon tomorrow."

At that moment the front door imploded, red and blue lights flashed on patrol cars in the driveway, uniformed men rushed forward with guns drawn. That night Roger, Norma, Jason and Christine were all 'Heroes of the Day.'

REVENGE OF THE SALMON

3010 A.D. was a dreadful year. During the last century, the earth had undergone massive changes. The severe climate changes in the period 2010 to 2040, resulted in massive flooding. Entire cities were devastated. Volcanic eruption, after volcanic eruption darkened the sky.

Clouds of volcanic ash over the long period reduced sunlight to less than ten percent. Air travel, in fact all transportation became increasingly difficult and finally impossible. Temperatures began to drop. All crops failed. A mini- ice age occurred. Animals and people starved or froze to death. Governments collapsed. Civilization ceased to function.

The people who endured fought each other to the death for survival.The final tribe remaining was the family of David Suzuki III. He and his extended family moved to the extreme southern part of Costa Rica, in the province of Carpi, next to Panama.

Their grandfather, David Suzuki, was the eminent naturalist turned doomsday philosopher. Wisely, he prepared for his family, by carefully selecting the safest region in the world. He constructed a virtual fortress of concrete buildings heated with thermal energy piped from the earth's hot springs. The same heat generated electrical energy enough to light the enclave.

He stockpiled provisions including several tons of wheat, rice, and corn in dry form. He also stored equal amounts of canned and dried vegetables, fruits, and meats. He allowed for enough provisions for twenty people for 80 years.To date 19 members ate through the provisions, none could be grown in its' place.

The family was down to a single survivor, Linda Suzuki. She had just watched her husband dying. He refused to eat for the past two months leaving the remaining meager food for Linda and the others.

This was the final day. Linda picked up her fork, scooping the last bit of pacific coast pink salmon from the Gold Seal can.

Looking out at the lifeless landscape it reminded her of past satellite pictures from the Mars explorer program.

She had no options. With a heavy heart, she took an overdose of sleeping pills, set aside for this moment. She then lay down beside her husband, and turning out the light; she tugged the covers over them both for the final time. The human race was irrevocably extinct.

Two months later two thousand miles to the north, the sunshine battled through the mist. It was September 15, and the Pacific sockeye salmon were starting their spawning run up the mighty Columbia River. The salmon too suffered the devastation heaped on the earth. A few were saved only by the somewhat more moderate ocean temperatures.

The run this year would number only 200 fish. They would be laying 500,000 eggs. Of those 100,000 fish would reach maturity to return in 4 years. Within 8 years, the returning run would be over a million fish.

3010 was a good year, for the salmon. The future appeared promising.

MY JOB INTERVIEWS

"All aboard for Edmonton, Jasper, Kamloops, and Vancouver," blared out the Saskatoon C.N.R. station public address system. A single tear ran down my mother's cheek, as I boarded the train.

With my high school diploma in my back pocket, I said goodbye to the small Central Saskatchewan farming community that had been home. At nineteen, it was time to cut the apron strings.

Soon I was aboard, and underway, with the familiar click, click of the train wheels passing over rail joints. Watching the frozen countryside zip by, my thoughts wandered back to the life I was leaving behind. Friends, relatives, some three generations strong, all living in close harmony, sharing the meager resources the unforgiving prairie produced. Was it a hard life? Yes, yet it was filled with memories, of neighbor helping neighbor, social gatherings, weddings, holidays, baseball tournaments and church socials. No one was ever excluded.

It was December 1. Harvesting was completed a month ago, as shown by the stubble, left on the grain fields. Early morning frost now clung on tree branches. Threatening black clouds hung in the air. Snowflakes dotted the air. Huge flocks of swift flying wild ducks and Canada geese were flying southward, hours ahead of the first heavy snowfall. Ice filled country road ruts paralleled the train tracks. The local sloughs were frozen over with newly built muskrat houses dotting their surfaces. A few stubborn ducks huddled on the icy shores, resting for an hour or two before continuing their southerly migration.

As the train ride progressed, past school Christmas concerts came to mind. The popularity of the teacher was measured by the quality and entertainment value of that year's concert content. In many cases that dictated as to whether the teacher's contract would be renewed the following year. My cheeks still burned with embarrassment, I remembered the fourth grade. Due to a shortage of female students, I was required to play the part of Mable, in a skit portraying the local area women. There I sat in a tartan patterned winter coat, a blond wig made from woven binder twine; pants rolled up under the coat, on my feet a pair of high heels.

I was knitting away while gossiping back and forth to the other "women." I will tell you as a 10 year old, I was hoping someone would appear and take over that god-awful part. Some years later Dustin Hoffman's "Tootsie" was a big hit perhaps my effort set the stage for that. There I was, the brunt of laughs; the subject of much finger pointing. The skit was enjoyed by the men whose wives we humorously portrayed. The men being the school trustees were more than satisfied with the concert, so Miss Olexan, thereby cleverly managed to keep her position for a further two years.

Thanks to that performance, my father also delayed the age at which I was allowed to drive the tractor, perhaps he thought my knitting skills would interfere with operating the farm equipment.

During the next nine hours on the train, I absorbed my time reading a timely book given to me by mother. It was the 1937edition of Dale Carnegie's "How to Make Friends and Influence People" Being an avid reader, I had it mostly read by the time the train arrived in Edmonton. Needless to say, I was anxious to test the theory of making friends.

Across from me sat a man in his fifties, dressed in green denim worker's clothes, cowboy hat tilted to the right and pushed up, and a cigarette dangling from the corner of his mouth. The

Zane Grey, western novel "Riders of The Purple Sage" rested on the seat beside him. *"He will do."* I smiled, smiling being the first rule in the book

"Hi there" I ventured "how are you doing? How far are you going?" Showing interest was the second rule.

He glanced at the book on my lap, no doubt aware of the title; tentatively he replied, "Fine son, my name is Mike. I live in Jasper, and will be getting off there"

"Rob here, pleased to meet you Mike. What work do you do in Jasper?"

"I have an animal control contract with the parks department, mostly bears"

"Very interesting, do you shoot many of them?"

"No, no nothing like that! When we see one too close to town, I fire a shotgun blast over the bear's head, then the dogs chase the bear for a couple of miles. If they come back into town we repeat it again."

"What if the bear keeps coming back over and over?"

"Then we live trap him and relocate him so far into the wilderness where his own mother couldn't find them." He said chuckling.

"Have any bears turned on you?" My imagination was running wild. "I hear they can be dangerous"

"An old toothless grizzly sow once charged me."

"Golly gee wiz what did you do?" I was picturing the danger he had found himself in.

His eyes lit up, he winked, smiled and he added. "I had this pet Sasquatch, Romeo, at the time. Romeo stepped between us, grabbed the bear by the neck, pinned her to the ground and thrashed the daylights out of her, right there on the edge of town. That bear stood up and limped away, I never saw her again. The Mounties reported seeing her up near Revelstoke one hundred fifty miles west of Jasper.

Realizing, he must have shot the bear, but substituted a

manufactured explanation to keep things from getting morbid, I smiled and nodded. I looked down at my book wondering if a logical answer was available. Looking up, I improvised. "Nice try, you really had me going there, for a couple of minutes".

I had made a friend during the next two hours we chatted about every topic, from goose hunting tales, giving the cunning geese supernatural powers at avoiding hunters, to condemning the cold weather, to complaining about the sandwiches being sold on the train. Mike left the train in Jasper around about two A.M. From the window, I saw his wife meet him, along with two huge Bernese mountain dogs. These were no doubt his famous bear chasing team.

As first light appeared, I marveled at the height of the Rocky Mountains, sometimes having to bend down to floor level to see the peaks. The people nearby give me inquisitive looks, wondering just what was happening as I doubled over to get a good view. Without comment, I grinned back. As the train dropped in elevation animals began appearing, a moose here, an elk there, even an elusive mountain sheep. I had read about mountain sheep in various sport-hunting magazines, as to their superior eyesight, wisdom and rock climbing abilities.

The train screeched to a steaming halt in Vancouver at ten AM Sunday. It was a nice clear sunny warm day. There to greet me was my cousin Frank, smiling jovially, showing me to his car and off we went for a quick tour of Vancouver. He drove down West Broadway, past the Bowman GMC lot with its impressive neon sign. It was more than 30 feet high. He continued, over the Burrard Street Bridge, down Georgia Street, onto the Stanley Park seawall drive, straight to Prospect point.

There I had my first view of the Pacific Ocean, in fact my first view of any ocean. The water was dead calm,

"Where are the thirty foot waves?" I questioned, recalling my grandfather's wall back on the prairies having a huge painting depicting sailors scrambling to keep their vessel from being overwhelmed by massive waves. "Some days we may get two foot waves' replied Frank "no thirty footers here".

Monday morning came; my search for career opportunities took me down to the Pacific Press building, home of the Vancouver Sun. It was early, seven A.M. I began strolling around the various streets to pass the time away. At eight the doors opened, in I went. "I am looking for work," I announced to the young woman, her nametag identified her as Melissa. She was standing at the counter, uncovering her Underwood typewriter. "Personnel is upstairs, on the third floor" she replied, misunderstanding my intentions.

"No, no, I wish to place an ad in the work wanted section of your paper, the Vancouver Sun." I had scanned Saturday's classified section for the correct ad number.

She put a sheet in her typewriter, saying, "Go ahead sir." I quickly instructed her, having committed the ad to memory the night before. "High school graduate, nineteen, seeks work. Rob TR4-2149".

"Are you sure that all you want to say?" She obviously expected more than a two-line ad.

"Yes, thank you that should do the trick," I assured her pretending I knew what I was doing. "There's nothing like a dynamite ad," I added, regretting the words as soon as I had spoken. She took my payment of two dollars eighty-five cents, for the four day classified placement.

"Your ad will appear in tomorrow's Vancouver Sun "she replied. "By the way, good luck with that" Melissa quipped, as I turned to leave.

Surely, Melissa thought I was one brick short of a full load. I hastened towards the revolving door, almost tripping myself, as I rotated around and stumbled out onto the street.

Tuesday 10, A.M, the ad was in the paper, as we wrote it up. It was begging for attention, every word correct. I had been sitting beside the phone for two hours visualizing exactly how to handle the many calls I would surely get. "Ring," there it was! I waited until the second ring, "no reason to appear overly anxious, "Hello Rob here" I excitedly hollered into the receiver, not quite as I had practiced. A polished voice replied. This is Mr. Morgan. I'm the manager of Kingsway Premium Auto Sales; I'm calling about your advertisement."

"The one in the Sun?" I questioned without thinking, knowing well, there was no other ad. I felt somewhat overwhelmed and somewhat embarrassed simultaneous.

"Why yes "confirmed Mr. Morgan sensing immediately he had the edge on sophistication. "How long have you been in town?" He chortled, guessing correctly that I was not a Vancouverite. "How long are you staying?"

"I've been here over four days now. I arrived on the CNR from Saskatoon on Wednesday morning. Jobs in Saskatchewan are rarer than robins in December."

"Sounds like you had an exciting trip," chuckled Mr. Morgan 'Would you come to my office for an interview, perhaps we can help you out", he crooned. "How about this afternoon at two o'clock? We are at 145 Kingsway, do you know where that is?"

"Two sounds fine, and yes I am only eight blocks from your location. Thank-you, I will be there." I was beaming with joy, thinking about all the money that I would save on bus fare by being able to walk to work. At fifty cents a day that would be over one hundred twenty-five dollars a year! How lucky can a guy get? Smiling I ended the call. Then I ran upstairs to brush my teeth, shower and put on my one suit, the one from my recent high school graduation.

Promptly at one thirty, there I was sitting on the bus stop bench directly across from the Kingsway Sales lot. Deciding to do a little investigating of the lot and the surrounding area, I saw several car lots lined the street on both sides. They were all owner operated, non-franchise businesses, each vying to lure customers with exaggerated sales sign slogans. One said 'We

Make Friends First, Then We sell Them Cars For Life." Another boasted 'Our Cars Are Triple Inspected By Government Trained Mechanics." Yet another stated. "You Don't Drive Our Cars, You unleash Them."

Kingsway's was more modest "Check The Rest, Then Buy From The Best." Another dealer message sign stated "Why go elsewhere and be cheated, come here first". A repair shop next to that, not to be out done boldly displayed "Auto repair service, try us once and you will never go anywhere again." I chuckled at that one.

Counting the inventory of cars at Kingsway, I was amazed. Forty six cars, again my math skills began calculating "that's forty-six cars at an average price of at least one thousand dollars a car. That would be forty six thousand dollars." These guys are loaded," I thought, as I walked across the street to find the seemingly successful MR. Morgan.

"Come on in, I'm Mr. Morgan," boomed the silk suited tall man, as he came walking from the private office, out into the waiting room. "You must be Rob?"

Nodding I shook his extended hand. "Yes sir, how are you? It is a real pleasure to meet you Mr. Morgan," I continued." It is nice weather we are having." All prairie people mention weather conditions first and foremost. It would be rude not to, then you mention the crops. Being it was December in the city, I decided to skip the crops part. "How has your health been Mr.Morgan?" It was again customary to cover the health issue also."

Good, good," replied, Mr.Morgan, declining any further comment on his health. "Come in and have a seat; we will fill out an application." He reached into his desk drawer and whipped out a one page form handing it to me." Fill in as much as you can. He lit up a cigarette, leaned back in his chair and began watching me fill in the spaces on the form. After ten minutes, the form was completed and Mr. Morgan took it back, leaned back again in his high back chair and scanned the information.

"This looks fine, we need someone on the lot who can start as a lot attendant, learn the basics of cars and then began selling. I would say in six or seven months you will be earning up to a thousand a month. How does that sound?"

I was ready to kiss him. "Sounds fine to me." I was grinning from ear to ear. In my mind, I thought of my cousin Gordy back in Saskatoon working for a bank at only two hundred a month. "A thousand a month within six months sounds pretty good, does that mean I have the job?"

"Just one small detail, Rob," Mr.Morgan, smiled in a fatherly way.

"What would that be sir?" *He probably needs a reference or character letter*, I thought to myself. That would be no problem; I could get one from the manager of the co-op outlet back home. He knew me well. His phone number was in my wallet.

"The position requires that you have a vehicle, do you own a car now?"

"No"

"Not to worry, we have some excellent units in stock right now. How much money have you to spend?" My smile disappeared. I was beginning to feel like a pail of oats in a horse barn.

"Well I was not figuring on buying a car just yet! I will have to give this some thought." My only thought was *"where is the door, how do I get the hell out of here"*

Mr.Morgan kept pressing. "We have a 1958 Sunbeam Alpine Sportster here that would suit you. It will really impress the women in your life! It's on at twelve hundred. However, being a staff member, you can knock two hundred right off the top. How does that sound?"

Knowing I only had a total of four hundred eighty two dollars to my name, I was just about ready to bolt. This was way over my head. A séance was not needed to realize what was going down The last thing I wanted to do, right now, did not include test driving the Sunbeam or impressing women. *The "thousand a month"* was just more *horse feathers,* I surmised. Up I stood, extending my hand to Mr. Morgan. Thank you for your time sir. I will call you in a day or so if I decide to take your offer"

"Don't wait too long, I have several more applicants coming in later today," the ever smiling Mr.Morgan added. His insistence was not making me change my mind. "Keep us in mind, mention us to your friends" was all I heard as I crossed the door sill,

I continued on, almost walking into the Sunbeam, as I rushed down towards the street. In my mind, I could visualize myself buying a car today and being fired on Tuesday. Someone else could experience that embarrassment.

Upon arriving home, I was staying with my Aunt and Uncle, they laughed at the recounted afternoon activities They all assured me, I had done the right thing.

That afternoon a second call came in from a funeral director, "This is the manager of Forest Grove Funeral Home. Would you be interested in learning our business?"

"I have to think about this for a moment," I started to say. Then, with the moment over, I continued. "Sure I would like to hear about your business. May I come and see you tomorrow at ten a.m.?"

"Actually, four would be better, as we have a service at ten and another at two. We can't keep the customers waiting you know," he jokingly commented.

"Yes, I understand, four o'clock it is, I will see you then." He give me his telephone number and address on East 8th Ave.

The call did bolster my confidence. I drew comfort from knowing there was apparently a huge demand for trainees. After the car sales fiasco, it would be interesting to talk to a business that dealt ethically with people. From what I knew of the funeral business back home, it was the most respected business going.Never could I imagine a funeral business ever trying to rip anyone off, unthinkable.

This funeral business thing must have impacted my mind, for that night, the most realistic dream I ever experienced occurred. There I was in the back room of the funeral parlor, you know, the room where they prep you, before dressing you all up and powdering your face. This body was stretched out face up, on a stainless steel table, covered with a white sheet, "Who could this be?" I wondered, in my dream.

In marched a white coated man with two containers of fluid in his hands. He walked up to the table, set down the containers and whipped the sheet off the body. Well I almost fainted, if such a thing is possible while dreaming. It was me on the table. "Just a darn minute here!" I wanted to holler. "I'm supposed to be working here. Where is the manager? "At that moment I awoke in a cold sweat. This always happens in my dreams, just when things get explained you wake up. You never relive the exact same dream, so you can find out what happened. Anyhow the clock indicated five a.m." "That's enough of this bullshit, I'm getting up" I exclaimed, realizing I was very much alive, even if a bit rattled.

Dressing for the interview later that afternoon, took some thought. My suit was black, good there. A black tie was in order, no problem with that. Black shoes, shined and ready. I left the house looking like a young Zorro; the only thing missing was the black mask, cape, gloves and sword.

The funeral home was immaculately landscaped. I entered the door marked "Office" and timidly shuffled up to the glass counter, which contained below within it various vase like containers for cremation remains. There was even one made of a soluble material. If your deceased wanted to be disposed of at sea, in a lake or thrown in a river, you merely chucked this container of ashes into the water. In about four minutes it was at the bottom disintegrating.

A shiver went up my spine as I pounded on the desk bell to announce my arrival. A distinguished gray haired gentleman came out of the back office; on the door it had printed "Mr. Harold Winston." On his suit was a name tag" Mr. Winston. "Mr. Winston?" I questioned, heaven knows who else he could have been.

He extended his hand "Come on in Rob." quite remarkably he knew instantly who I was. The fact I was standing clued him in.

"Don't sit down," he added. "We are going to show you around first."

"Sounds good," I lied, knees shaking, face whitening, no longer smiling, "what am I doing here?" I thought "reliving last night's dream ?".

Seeing my discomfort he remarked "You will be fine, just follow me", he continued "I started here some twenty years ago, just like you." Through the chapel we marched, the janitor was rearranging things after the two o'clock service. Flower arrangements were everywhere "must have been a well liked guy," I thought as we passed by.

As we proceeded further, past the small alter, into the next hallway to the back of the building, I had an inkling what was coming next. I was right "this is our preparation room" proudly stated Mr. Winston, "you will be spending a lot of your time in here learning the procedures." In we went, there it was, the dreaded stainless steel table, containers of chemicals stored below, all ready for the next client. The distinctive smell of formaldehyde seemed familiar. It was the same chemical we sprayed on our seed grain back home so the bugs wouldn't eat the kernels before they germinated The concrete floor was painted with blood red floor enamel. The reason was clear, a drain situated in the middle of the floor lay ready, coiled up on the wall was a flushing hose, exhaust fans whirled away overhead. Very little was left to the imagination, *"nothing I can't get used to, after all I was a farm boy,"* I reasoned.

For the next twenty minutes he explained at length the preparation procedures, nothing was left out. It was so clear, he could have been quoting directly from a manual, word after word, describing what to do next, finally the presentation was over.

"What do you think of things so far?" he inquired. My gills were turning green, my eyes kept glancing towards the exit, my feet ready to follow.

"Pretty qu-quiet dow-down here eh" was all I could muster. "How long does it take to, to, to pre-prepare the bod-bod-body? Years ago, I had the propensity for stuttering, when ill at ease. I was back in that mode here.

"Three or four hours, unless it is an accident victim then you can double the time. We get extra pay for that. But do not worry you can play the radio while you work, except when there are services upstairs."

"Yes, a rad-rad-radio would-would., hel-help "I glanced towards the door once more. "Be a man for God's sake," I admonished myself, feeling ill.

"We can go back to the office now." Mr. Winston offered seeing I was stressed." We will go over your hours, pay and benefits." He was getting bad vibes from my reaction to the "prep" room. Perhaps he recalled his first experiences there as a trainee.

Seated back in the office, a call came in. With no other staff around Mr. Winston answered. "Forest Grove, we are here to help you." I could only hear his side of the conversation,

"Very sorry to hear that Mrs. Gilroy, yes I remember, you were in with Henry about two months ago making pre-arranging. I liked him the moment you stepped through the door. He was a first class gentleman. Yes, I am most sorry to hear he has left us. When did you think you wanted to schedule the service? For, Friday perhaps? Yes Friday will be doable, in fact I am just hiring more staff today." He glanced my way to gauge my reaction. I tried to look somber, arranging funerals was serious business.

"Come by tomorrow afternoon, at four, and we will go over the final details. Henry would have wanted that. We will also

issue a receipt for your payment at that time," he discreetly hint-
ed. He finished with "please convey my sympathy to the children and grandchildren, Henry talked so fondly of them. He
will be missed. Thanks for calling Mrs. Gilroy." There was a
pause, "yes I can call you Nancy, thanks again Nancy."

With that he hung up and made a notation in his appointment diary. He looked my way saying "excuse me." I must make
one more call, he dialed a number. "Tony, this is Harry, slip
down to Vancouver general and pick up Mr. Gilroy, from room
610,they are expecting you in fifteen minutes. When you get
back and drain him, just stick him in the cooler for now, his
wife is coming in tomorrow and we will try to upgrade his ar-
rangement from a simple cremation to the deluxe service. By
the way Tony don't forget you and Fiona are coming over for
dinner tonight with Mildred and me. No you don't have to
bring anything, we have a good wine cellar, and flowers are no
problem as you know, see you then".

I was seeing two sides to this man, the work related sympathy jargon, and then the "this is just another day at the office"
side., "This guy is not much different from a car salesman," I
concluded "out to get all he can."

He redirected his attention giving me the lowdown on the
hours, suggesting there would be some night work involved,
"that should be fun." I thought sarcastically, thinking back to
the" prep room." The starting salary would be three hundred
dollars monthly, with increases every 6 months, not that bad
compared to other training positions.

"I will give you a call tomorrow at quarter to four" I promised
as I stood up shook hands and stepped out into the early evening rush hour, inhaling the fresh evening air wondering just
how to handle this offer.

The next morning a third call came in. A public accountant, Mr.Magazin was looking for a trainee.,I accepted the interview for eleven the same day, filled with anticipation, as to

what the duties would be.I remembered the town clerk back home helping the surrounding area farmers and small businessmen file their accounts each spring, with the dreaded income tax office located in Saskatoon.

Mr. Magasin the practitioner was a slight, wiry man in his sixties, with a heavy French accent, nervous as hell, hands shaking, talking a mile a minute, a cup of coffee half consumed, obvious not his first of the day. He had operated a small accounting, income tax practice at this location for twenty years now. He needed help immediately, his most recent assistant, who had been with him two months, had failed to come to work on Monday, three days ago, without explanation, the busy tax preparation season was approaching "I need someone more reliable," commented Mr. Magasin. "I am done with him, his mother talked me into giving him a chance, look how he repays me!"

I felt I had to answer in some form, "maybe he would rather sell cars," I replied.

"Perhaps so, let's forget about him shall we," he barked, seeming annoyed by the whole thing.

In the small one room office, he quickly explained the intricate aspects of the job, the accounting courses, tax subjects, and basic economic principle courses I would have to take by correspondence at night and on weekends, while working for him during the day. Before the interview was finished Mr. Magasin was showing me double entry bookkeeping steps, entries that were made in special journals, totaled and balanced.

I was intrigued, having sat behind a desk for twelve years, this all felt comfortable, as well as interesting. I was hired and at work the next day, loving every day I went to work. So began my accounting career which spanned some 40 years

The next day I informed Mr. Winston, at the funeral home of my choice not to accept his offer. He agreed that the funeral business was not for everyone. "See you soon," he offered, as he ended the call. Was he predicting my future? I quickly hung up.

LIFE IN THE SIXTIES

SALESMAN OF THE WEEK

Eric had just graduated, and jobs were scarce. He was ready to go back to the family farm and hang his diploma on the outhouse wall.

After three months of filling out dozens of applications and attending countless job interviews, he was disenchanted. Disenchanted with the nine to five jobs he was not getting.

Scanning the news classified, he saw the advertisement in the Morning Sun News. It read:

Junior Sales Position, Earn $ 500 Weekly, Must have car and be willing to travel. Phone TR4-VACU.

Eric was attracted by the ad; he felt it suited him in every respect. $ 500 a week was excellent pay. He had a car, if a 1952 Chevy Blair qualified. Travel was his middle name.

It all appeared perfect. Following up on the opportunity, he dialed the number. He got an immediate response.

"Energizer Vacuum Company how may we help you?"

He answered back. "I'm calling about the junior sales position."

"One moment please. I will connect you to our President, Mr. Walker. May I say who is calling?"

"Eric Goodenough" Eric felt important. He would be talking with the President of the company.

"Scotty Walker here, Mr. Goodenough. I understand you're interested in the junior sales position?"

"You bet. I'm your man, sir." Eric said replying enthusiastically.

"Fine, fine," Scotty sidestepped Eric's comment. "First things first, I need you to come in for an interview; how about tomorrow morning at nine?"

"Nine is suitable, I will see you then. Thank you." Eric felt the job was practically his. He was already making plans, imagining how he was going to be spending his first pay cheque.

Promptly at five minutes to nine Eric was at their door. The sign in the window proudly displayed "Energizer Vacuum Company Ltd". Behind the plate glass window were displayed several sparkling stainless steel canister vacuum machines, looking as attractive as puppies at a pet store.

Eric approached the receptionist. "I'm Eric Goodenough, here for the job interview."

Speaking into the intercom, the receptionist announced, "Mr. Walker your appointment is here." Turning to Eric, she smiled. "Go right in, it's the first door on your right."

Eric entered the impressive executive office. The left wall had numerous framed sales achievement awards. The ivory colored plush carpeting contrasted with the dark walnut desk. A handsome crescendo was positioned behind a black leather upholstered high back chair.

A tall well-dressed man rose and walked briskly around the desk, right hand extended. "How are you Eric? I'm Scotty Walker. I'm pleased to meet you. Come in have a seat."

"Thank you for this interview." Eric said, taking a seat.

"Now, young man, let's get down to business." Mr. Walker was all business. Studying Eric's resume for a few minutes, he looked up. "Have you any sales experience? More precisely, have you done any door to door sales?"

"Only a limited amount. In Scouts, we had and annual

drive selling Planters peanuts door to door. I did that for four years."

"An early starter eh?" Mr. Walker grinned. "How did you do compared to your other fellow scouts?"

"About twice as well. I sold the product in three out of four calls."

"A 75% closing rate that's great. We have a training program, covering a couple of days. We send you out as an assistant and observer, so you can learn about the machines, learn how to handle objections from prospects and close sales." Scotty Walker continued. "It gives you a chance to see if you can handle the public. It gives us a chance to asses your suitability for the position."

"That sounds agreeable to me; I intend to work hard at this."

"Good, you start on Monday? You'll be working with Doug Wilmot. Meet him here at 9:30."

"Will do, see you then." Eric rose to leave "Thanks again, for this opportunity."

Monday morning saw Eric arriving eager and willing to learn.

"Hi young fellow." Doug Wilmot greeted him "So you, want to learn the ins and outs of the vacuum business, do you?

"As fast as possible." Eric smiled back.

"O.K then, help me load my van with these machines and supplies, and we'll hit the road."

They drove to the designated area of South Devon, an upscale area of the city, Doug give him important pointers. "We sell by demonstrating the machines, offering to clean their sofa, the car interior, even the dog's sleeping mat. The key is to get the owner's permission to do a demonstration. That's the start of the presentation; after that the machines sell themselves."

They reached Devon, looked at the list of appointments. They had been generated from the coupons that customers had filled out at last week's home show. He drove to the first address shown.

Mrs. Millie March was the first prospect. The house was the most modest one on the block. Possibly, Mrs. March wanted to show the neighbors some glitter. A new vacuum would do that. The appointment was for ao a.m.. It was 10 minutes to "game time".

Eric unloaded the demo machine while Doug strolled up to the door and rang the bell. He had a "gift" in his left hand consisting of a bottle of lemon scented furniture oil spray, made in China, cost to Energizer fifty five cents. It was a very important icebreaker.

Mrs. March, promptly opened the door, dressed in an immaculate blue pantsuit, hair in a ponytail, and low heeled shoes. She was looking forward to the visit. "Right on time fellows" she chirped. "Come on in."

"I'm Doug; this is my assistant Eric, Mrs. March. We are pleased to meet you. Here is a little something to thank you for agreeing to a demonstration." He handed her the furniture spray. "Where do you want us to set up?"

"I thought we could have you do the sofa in the family room."

"Perfect, Eric plug in over against the wall there."

"Now Mrs. March, this unit here is our latest and most reliable unit, the XL700. It will compare with any built in vacuum anywhere. To demonstrate we will put a Kleenex between the lower pipe and the vacuum head and show you why."

After 5 minutes of vacuuming, Doug ordered Eric to stop. He took the head off the vacuum pipe and lowered the dust laden Kleenex onto the coffee table. There rested a sizable ball of gray dust, two inches in diameter.

"This shows the suction power in this little baby." Doug patted the machine.

"How much?" blurted out Mrs. March, hardly able to contain her excitement.

"This week, they are Seven Hundred and Ninety dollars."

"Is it guaranteed?"

"For three years, and all included in the price."

"I'll take it," beamed Mrs. March. Doug smiled and nodded

"Is a personal cheque O.K.," inquired Mrs. March

"Good as Gold, make it out to Energizer Vacuum Company Ltd."

They demonstrated two more units and sold one more to a homeowner, just three doors down from the March residence.

On the way back to the store Doug explained the commission structure to Eric. "I made a 15 % commission on those two units which gives me a total of $ 225. That is not bad for less than three hours of work eh?"

Eric agreed that this could be the right career for him.

"Tomorrow, we will send you out on your own, with a handful of leads and see how you do. You can phone ahead today and set up the appointments. Space them out about one hour apart." Doug turned the van around and started back to the office.

Eric had his lunch and set about phoning his list of prospects. Out of the six leads he secured three appointments for the next day.

At 9.30 the next morning he walked briskly up the sidewalk to ring Mrs. Peel's doorbell. A German Sheppard dog sat near the front step. Eric whispered "Hi Pup" and stepped up to ring the doorbell.

All hell broke loose as soon as the dog heard the ringing doorbell. The dog leaped forward, biting Eric in the upper thigh. Eric jumped back, trying to put distance between himself and the dog.

Mrs. Peel opened the door just in time to see the dog make another move towards Eric, who by now was facing the dog, with the vacuum cleaner he was carrying held strategically between him and the dog. "Down Thunder, get back." She ordered the dog away. He slunk a few feet away still watching Eric intently "I'm ever so sorry, are you hurt? "She asked.

"Just startled," replied Eric, his leg on fire. With, his pants torn, he limped into the foyer. "No harm done," he added, try-ing to minimize the incident.

The demonstration went smoothly. Mrs. Peel was very coop-erative. She was still sorry for the dog attack. Within 15 minutes she interrupted Eric's Kleenex presentation "I'll take two. One for me, and one for my son Victor. He has an apartment down town." In short order the units were in her possession and Eric was walking out the door with a $ 1500.00 cheque on his clip-board. The dog waged his tail in a friendly goodbye manner, as Eric departed.

"Don't do that again." Eric warned him in a whisper as he hurried by.

On his way to the next appointment, he stopped at a park washroom and fixed the tear in his pants by applying some duct tape from the inside and pressing the torn edges down. For good measure in case of bleeding, he put a piece of Kleenex over the black bruised area of his thigh and applied more duct tape.

Prospect number two was Mr. Laird, an old age pensioner. He had retired three years ago, from his last position as a mine superintendent in the Yukon. He appeared to be, lonely, and still trying to adjust to his boring ,retirement lifestyle.

Eric reached out towards his doorbell, taking a quick look over his shoulder to see if there are any dogs in the vicinity, all clear. Before he had a chance to ring the bell, the door opens and Mr. Laird greeted him "You must be the vacuum salesman," he said, grinning at Eric.

"Right on sir, by the way my name is Eric"

"Come in; come in, how about a coffee? It's all ready, come in the kitchen." For the next hour Mr. Laird talked about his life as a mine superintendent. He had been all over North America. After having several accidents he had to retire early due to a lung problem associated with work. Eric sat there smiling and nodding in agreement with everything being said. He remem-bered his instructions about selling. "*If the customer wants to talk let him go at it"* Finally Mr. Laid interrupted himself "Gee it's noon I guess you have work to do?"

"Yes, sir, I would like to demonstrate the machine. Where shall I set up?"

"Never mind that," replied Mr.Laird

Eric thought he had lost the sale "Don't you want a demonstration?"

"Son if I can run a mine with 200 employees, I think I can read the operating manual for your gismo there. Go get me a new one from your car, and tell me how much I owe you.

"Yes Sir" Eric disappeared for two minutes then reappeared, with a new machine.

"If I have any problems I can always call you over," suggested Mr. Laird.

Eric made a mental note to be sure to have some free space in his day for the next few weeks. Mr. Laird was going to be calling; Eric had no doubt about that.

In fifteen minutes Eric was off to lunch, his company another $ 750 dollars richer.

"What a stroke of luck this job is." he whistled to himself as he wheeled into Taco Time for lunch. "One more call at 1.30, then a few phone calls to set up tomorrow's prospects, and I am done for the day."

At 1.30 he was on the doorstep of Mr. and Mrs. Dartmouth's residence. "What a lovely house" Eric thought, as he stopped in the circular drive bordered with colorful flowers.

Stopping the car, he spotted two cats on the front door mat. "Should be safe here" he mused, still thinking of the dog attack earlier.

He rang the doorbell without incident, the cats moved over under the Japanese cherry tree. The door opened to a woman in her mid to late seventies. Her husband was hanging four steps behind. It was obvious who would be making the decisions here.

"Mrs. Dartmouth? Hi I'm Eric Goodenough from Energizer"

"Come in Eric, I'm Elsie, we were expecting you. This is my husband Harry.

Eric was glad to get back to work. He set things up, demonstrating the vacuum on the living room sofa for only for two or three minutes. He did not want to upset the woman of the house by showing her too much dirt on the Kleenex.

He turned the machine off and undid the head. There was about one-third the dust he normally would collect, just enough to show the suction power of the unit, but not enough to draw her ire.

"You keep a very clean house Mrs. Dartmouth! I must say this is the cleanest house I've ever seen! "He didn't mention that he had only been in five others so far."

She purred at the stroking comment. "It would be even cleaner if Harry didn't put his dirty feet up on that end of the sofa when he watches T.V." She glared at Harry momentarly.

Eric was now contemplating just who to address when closing the deal. He decided to try Harry, figuring a little reverse psychology would land him a sale. "How about it Harry, are you going to buy the little woman here a new vacuum?"

Harry was hesitating. "Maybe we should think about it over night and give you a call tomorrow, how about that?"

Before Eric could reply Mrs. Dartmouth interjected "We'll take it. Harry go get your cheque book"

"Are you sure dear?" Harry was trying to regain the advantage.

"Eric thought he would ease Harry's mind "Under the consumer protection law you have ten days to cancel the contract, if for any reason you are not satisfied" Feeling he still had some face left, Harry threw Eric a thank you glance."

"We aren't canceling," Mrs. Dartmouth stressed emphatically, putting an end to Harry's recovery. The deal was done. She had her new vacuum and Eric was out the door with another $ 750.

The next day Eric decided to rent a suite from Mr. Laird.

Eric continued his sales career; he sold six more units that week. That earned him the 'salesman of the week' title in his first week. His future with the company looked bright. He was soon put on the permanent sales team.

On Monday morning, Mr. Laird was smiling, as Eric came in for his morning coffee

"Eric, I would like you to meet Carol, my niece from Calgary, she will be visiting me for a week."

"Very pleased to meet you Carol" Eric flashed his best sales smile "a lot can happen in a week."

THE FORTUNE TELLER

Eric needed answers, now. He had some important issues to clear up. Not that his life depended on it, not literally, but at the very least his life could be impacted greatly by the information he sought.

He had risen swiftly in the Energizer Vacuum Company, which was now a publicly traded Company, Eric was Vice President. The Company was being threatened with a lawsuit by a competitor.

His religious adviser, Reverend Underhill, had only generalities to offer, "Time will make the Lord's wishes clear to you, my son."

Eric thought, "I need more certainty then waiting for Divine intervention."

Eric's lawyer, Jack Kickyurass, was not much help either He was a self-proclaimed specialist in all matters. He knew everything about everything and everybody, a typical lawyer. However, this problem was one he would not over speculate on. All he would say is "we'll sue the bastards if they don't back off completely" What he really meant was, "if you think there is a chance to squeeze something for me out of this, I'm your man. Keep me in mind, I can always use the money."

Eric's accountant, Don Letsdolunch, was equally vague if not repetitious. "If they dare try that, I know this great lawyer, Jack Kickyurass, he'll see you get satisfaction. "Obvious the two were networking.

Eric was frustrated "Damit I'm going in circles here". He thanked Don and proceeded to the restaurant cashier. "That was a wasted thirty-five dollars," he mumbled, as he ponied up the lunch money.

He was convinced his problems were going to need supernatural powers to get him the right answers. He started going through the morning paper. There it was, right before his eyes in the 'Personal's' section.

"Psychic Readings, thirty minutes for thirty dollars.

Dial Delta Sapphire at 1-800- Get-Rich for an appointment".

"What can I lose? She's got to be more help than that greedy Kickyurass lawyer or that phony Letsdolunch accountant."

He telephoned his fiancé', Caro,l telling her of his plans. She acted somewhat hostile about the whole matter. "You're a prominent business executive Eric. Why do you need a psychic to tell you what to do?"

"Just to make sure honey, I like certainty." Eric replied, "A second opinion never hurts. In fact I may ask the psychic about our future as well."

"Oh well, now, really? You must be joking! Are you out of your mind?" Carol continued to rant "Sure let's base our entire future on some crackpot psychic" she was steamed, but then mellowed as she said goodnight. It was not like her to become disagreeable. In fact the reason Eric was attracted to her was because of her down to earth attitude. She was not at all pretentious, always supportive, well up to now. What you saw, she was. As Carol thought about it a bit longer, she hoped perhaps this "psychic visit" would prompt Eric into proposing. She would use this visit to her advantage.

The next day, Friday, August 13, at three thirty, Eric finally found the psychic's studio on the second floor, above a dry cleaning plant. He went through the cracked, dirty glass door leading up the grimy stairs, with peeling paint on either side of the staircase, spider cobwebs hanging like netting from every corner. At the top of the stairs a worn pathway in the hall rug led him to Suite "101" "Delta Sapphire PHD" it said on the door"

"PHD my eye" thought Eric "PHD must stand for "portable hand device" the crystal ball.

Eric entered the room. If the entry way and the stairway were below expectations, the inner office was not much better. A black cat hopped down from the waiting room chair and fled into its' makeshift cardboard "cat house" with the name 'Miller' scrawled above the cut out door. Incense fumes filled the air. Yet another odor lingered, one that suspiciously smelled like stale "marijuana" smoke.

The entire atmosphere practically cried out, in desperation, for improvements.

"Oh, what the hell," mumbled Eric. "I may as well see what she has to say." He rang the bell on the waist high linoleum covered counter. On the counter were three ashtrays filled to capacity with cigarette butts, chewed up Nicorette gum and Prozac wrappers. All presumably left by clients trying to calm their fears while waiting their turn.

"Never mind ringing" said a voice coming from a scruffy looking man seated behind an artificial palm plant. Eric had not noticed him in the poorly lit room. "She'll be with you as soon as she finishes with the client in there." He nodded towards a closed office door.

I'm her brother, Al. Coholics. I'm helping her out. I'm between jobs". His appearance clearly indicated he had been between jobs for at least twenty-five booze-filled years.

Hesitantly Eric took a seat. Moments later a middle-aged woman stormed out of the interview room, sobbing uncontrollably. Behind her unmistakably was the fortuneteller, Delta Sapphire, trying to console her about news the woman obviously did not want to hear. "I'm sorry honey, but you wanted the truth," she offered.

"You could have lied to me and told me something positive. Isn't that what all psychics do?. Telling me that since my husband is going broke and I should leave him is hard to take. Don't you have any feelings for people?"

"That's in you best interests, I would not be doing my job if you weren't told. You have to face the truth soon, you know."

"Never mind, give me a receipt. How much is that?"

"One hour is sixty dollars plus 12% tax total is sixty seven dollars and twenty cents."

"Do you take Visa?"

"Look around, do you see a Visa machine? The closest thing to metal is the cat's dish over there in the corner. Sorry, cash is all we deal in."

"Well all right then here is seventy" she handed the bills over "keep the change." She had calmed down by now. "May I see you the same time next week?"

"Sure Dear, whatever you want." Delta made a notation in her appointment book. The woman nervously headed for the door, shielding her face with a tissue.

Delta turned her attention to Eric. "Hi young fellow, your next." Eric followed her into the inner office. Delta was clad in a yellow colored Hawaiian Moo-Moo, decorated with big painted orange flowers, probably gotten from the nearby thrift store on senior's day. It nearly hid her 180 pounds of undulating fat. Her dirty blonde hair was up over her head, tightly wrapped up in a black nylon turban, making her a foot taller than her four foot four frame. Somewhere in the past she had an incisor tooth knocked out, leaving a noticeable gap when she smiled. "Some irate customer no doubt" he thought. Her appearance did not impress Eric. He was not one to give up.

He took a seat on the opposite side of Delta's old dust covered tablecloth. Sitting on the table was a Hollywood style "Crystal ball" that had seen better days. As a back up measure on the table there was a deck of cards, worn with ragged edges. All that was missing to complete the scene was a Quijie board.

Delta dimmed the main lights, then with both chubby hands wrapped around her crystal ball she started the session. "Now Eric how can I assist you?" In the dim light she flashed her toothless smile. Her eyes intently watched every facial expression Eric displayed, trying to get a "leg up" on his needs.

"I have two issues that need resolving." Eric decided to lay it all out on the table. "This conversation is confidential is it not?"

"Honey you secrets are safe with me." What she really meant was "safe" until she got home that evening and chatted with Ruby her next-door neighbor. "Tell me, what is your first problem?"

"I am the Vice president and a major shareholder in the company that manufactures Energizer Vacuum cleaners. We are currently heading into a legal dispute with National Vacuum Sales, who are threatening to launch a two million dollar lawsuit saying our product infringed on their patent. The vacuum they produce and sell, is called Excalibur Vacuum."

"How far along is this dispute?"

"We got a letter from their president Don T. Messwithme, ten days ago, advising us that they want a 20% royalty on all our sales for the past five years or they would launch legal action."

"How much would that 20% amount to?"

"Approximately one million dollars, we're talking serious dollars here."

"What does your lawyer advise?"

"To fight the bastards, sue them back for twice the amount."

Delta was not taken aback by the huge problem facing Eric and his company. "O.K. let's just see what the future holds for you." Delta dimmed the lights some more leaving only four flickering candles burning. She gazed deep into her crystal ball. The ball turned smoky gray, images darted in and out of the haze. Like graying goldfish, trying to escape their bowl.

After ten minutes, which seem like an hour to Eric, Delta looked up and smiled, bright eyes gleaming, sporting her good news look. "You don't have to worry any more about Excalibur Vacuum."

"Is that it? I don't have to worry about them, why not? Can you clarify that remark? I've got a million dollars at risk here."

"Mr. Don T. Messwithme will have bigger problems than his lawsuit against you, the law suit will never happen"

"How can you be so sure?"

"Just believe me, I know these things, after all I am a trained psychic. Trust me will you? Read the financial section of the Daily News this Friday, look under Legal Notices."

Delta did not tell him that the sobbing woman that preceded him was in fact, Mrs. Don T. Messwithme. She had just confided in Delta that the Excalibur Vacuum Co had been put into bankruptcy by the Bank. Delta advised her to divorce Don T. Messwithme and claim all the remaining assets, all of which were already in her name. Within one month Don T. Messwithme was going to be out on the street, penniless, a threat to no one.

Delta pressed on "What is you second problem? Let's put your mind at ease on that as well."

"Its not a problem. It is more of an uncertainty. I need to know if my fiancé Carol, and I are going to have a future together? We've been dating for five years now. I am not sure if we should get married and start a family?"

"What does Carol say?" Delta asked, trying to conceal a small smile.

"She wants me to make the final decision. She is letting me take the lead on this."

"Then we had better ask the Cards on this one, shall we."

Delta confidently switched off the crystal ball and picked up the playing cards. She used ordinary playing cards. From experience she knew clients had more confidence with cards they were familiar with, rather than the special Tarot cards. Giving them what appeared to be a quick Vegas style shuffle, Delta began placing them out on the table facing Eric.

"Ace of Hearts, looking good," Delta announced as she placed the first card. "This card indicates love, friendship, home and happiness. What a start!," she was getting excited. right along with Eric.

Then came a nine of hearts, Delta almost toppled from her chair. "My God, this is unbelievable!" she exclaimed "in twenty years this has only happened to me once before."

"What does it mean?" Eric was into it now, drawn in by Delta's antics.

"Hearts in addition to love, a 9 of hearts is a wish card,your desires will come true, this is absolutely astounding"

"Quick, play another card" Eric was on a roll. This was Las Vegas action, except love and happiness, not money, were the payoff.

"A six of spades, wow that means an improvement in your life, you are batting 1000."

"Another? Hurry."

"A six of diamonds, indicates an early marriage"

"Yet another?"

"A three of clubs, that means, a long engagement, then a fast wedding, a good marriage"

Eric and Carol had been engaged five years, it was time for decisive action.

That was enough. Eric suddenly knew what he had to do. "Five good predictions on five tries" this beats all odds of probability. Everything fell into place in his mind. "I've heard enough, I know what to do, let's leave it right there." Eric stood up, handed Delta two fifty dollar bills. "Thank you ever so much."

He was out the door, down the stairs, rushing down the street to Birk's Jewelry. He was going to purchase the ring today and propose to Carol that evening.

Delta made a quick call before ending the day. She had promised to call her client at 5 P.M. She dialed the number. "HI Carol, this is Delta, everything with Eric worked out just as we planned. You will be seeing him shortly."

She smiled, as she hung up the phone. She replaced the five key cards at the top of the deck, ready for tomorrow's readings. It had been a satisfying day. The cat, Miller, came out of his box and jumped on her lap. It was "Miller Time."

SIGN HERE PLEASE

Once upon a rainy night, a police car doing radar duty, stopped me. The constable approached my window. "Do you know you were doing 80 in a 40 zone?"

Naturally I had to disagree "80 sounds a little high, are you sure it wasn't 42?"

Ignoring that, he continued. "What's your hurry?"

"I didn't want to keep you waiting." I joked trying to lighten the conversation.

My philosophy is to make at least three people laugh every day. He declined to join in.

Playing hardball, he asked. "Have you been drinking?"

"Now, how would you define drinking?" I expected him to break out laughing.

Sternly, he elaborated. "Have you had any alcohol in the past six hours? His flashlight lit up my face.

"What time is it now? I have to accurately calculate when my six hours started."

"Look at your watch sir" For no apparent reason he was agitated.

"It stopped two years ago, I wear it for show. That's legal isn't it?"

"It's midnight. Now answer the question. Have you been drinking?"

"I've had one drink in the last six hours sir. It was a small one, real small. In fact I don't think I even finished it. You see, I did not want to impair my judgment. Yes, to be safe I poured half, maybe more of it down the sink."

That convinced him I was sober. A drunk could not have come up with such an artful story.

He wasn't giving up. "Can I see your driver's license ?"

"It's in my pocket, I doubt if you can see it from out there." Again I laughed ,alone.

"Just hand me your driver's license will you? "he barked, rain dripping off the brim of his hat. He took the license, checked it on his car computer, came back and began writing out a ticket.

"Just a minute there, don't you give warnings ?"

"Be quiet, you've had two speeding tickets in two weeks?" Now he was plain rude, just when I thought we were getting along so well.

"Who told you that? Isn't spreading that information around against my charter rights? Do I need a lawyer?"

"Just keep it up and you may need several," he replied. This guy knew his stuff.

"Can you recommend anyone?" If he had ever come across a good lawyer, I was most anxious to meet him.

"Just sign on the dotted line." He shoved the ticket and clipboard at me.

I decided to play dumb."What am I agreeing to if I sign this?"

"You're acknowledging receipt of the ticket."

"What if I don't sign?"

"I will call a wrecker, impound your car, you'll be walking home in the rain."

"Really, you can do that?"

"Watch me." He must have known Trudeau.

I signed on the dotted line.

"See you in court." I replied returning the clipboard.

"Looking forward to it sir." As he turned to walk away, his stern face was betrayed by a faint smile. Let's call it a laugh.

TO LITTER OR NOT TO LITTER

I hurried out of the woods towards my car, parked on the edge of the highway.

A solitary figure stood there in the fading light of early evening.

Raising a nightstick and pointing at me, he barked. "I'm Corporal Nelson, RCMP; keep your hands in sight, Mr. Rosewood." I assumed he had run my license numbers.

Half raising my arms," I enquired. "What's this about"?"

"I'll ask the questions. What were you doing in the woods?"

"Do I have to answer that?" I was getting annoyed.

"You aren't a hunter. Just tell me. What were you doing?"

"I was enjoying nature." I joked.

He didn't laugh. "Explain how did you did that?"

"I thought a walk in the woods would offer me some relief. I was feeling stressed"

"Be more specific. By relief do you mean you were toileting in the woods?"

He continued. "Did you do number 1 or number 2, or both?"

That was kids' slang. Was he talking down to me? "I wasn't looking for numbers. I told you I was relaxing for a minute or two."

"Littering in this park is an offence. Did you have a shovel and did you bury your crap?"

"Do you see a shovel?"

He glared "I Take it your answer is no?"

"Yes, it's no."

"Is that yes, you had no shovel, or no you didn't bury your excrement?"

I was being confused and felt bullied. I replied again, "Yes and no."

"I need a yes or a no answer, not both."

It was clear to me. "Yes I had no shovel, and no I didn't bury anything."

"That's better; now, I have to write you up for littering."

This was escalating into a confrontation. "I have a laptop, may I Google "littering "so we can agree on the definition?"

He glanced at his watch. "I'll give you five minutes."

Within 3 minutes my screen was screaming bad news. I read it out "*Littering- consists of the disposal, of waste products, without consent, in an inappropriate location.*"

It did not look promising for me. I changed my approach.

"Where is your bloody evidence?" I asked.

He countered. "Was blood involved? That adds hazardous waste to the charge!"

"Bloody, is just and English exaggeration."

"You did admit to littering?"

"No, I admitted to enjoying nature."

"How about your references to number 1 and number 2?"

"Number 1, was my stress from driving, and number 2, was a short walk in the woods."

"Are you now telling me, that you didn't drop your pants while sauntering in the woods?"

"No, I didn't and Yes, I didn't, either way, I'm in the clear."

It was dark by now. He would have to wait until morning to search for any evidence.

He sighed and closed his ticket pad. "You think you outsmarted me, don't you?"

"No, I don't think that." I was careful with my choice of words. "But yes, I do think I have reasonable doubt on my side."

"Are you a smart ass lawyer?"

"No, I'm not a smart ass and don't insult me by asking me if I'm a lawyer."

He began leaving, "I'll give you some advice Mr. Rosewood. In the future, carry some compostable bags with you."

I shut up and nodded.

BAD DAYS CAN BE GOOD DAYS

It was a memorable, as well, as a sad day.

Robert Collins, age 69, had sold his townhouse in suburban Vancouver after 8 years of retirement living with his late wife Sherry. They had been married 38 years.

Ruefully, he took down the pictures on the walls and separated them into two groups. The two he would keep and the 18 that would go to the Hospice Thrift store.

Fittingly it was raining outside, typical weather for November 15. The Subaru was packed with Robert's person belongings. A few clothes, his collection of books, a color T.V., a computer, a photo album and the two wall pictures.

The Hospice truck came and took away Sherry's personal effects, the furniture, the kitchen utensils, miscellaneous garage and gardening items as well as the 18 pictures.

The Re-max Realtor arrived to get the keys and arrange for a clean up crew to prepare the townhouse for the new owners.

Robert started up the Subaru, taking one final look at his unit through the rear view mirror, as he left the gated community.

He was heading one hour away, to the Maple Meadows retirement community, a senior complex of some 60 residents. He had secured a one-bedroom suite there with all services to be included ,from meals, to cleaning, to laundry. He had selected the Meadows ,as it offered nearby trails for nature walks,,as well as a small lake for shore trout fishing.

He drove slowly ,almost reluctantly, east, towards his new home. Past memories filled his mind as he motored his way through the countryside.

What did the future hold for him?

Deep in thought, Robert didn't notice the stop sign ahead and proceeded straight through the intersection. A car traveling in the cross road tried to avoid Robert's Subaru, but grazed the rear bumper as it passed through. Robert managed to keep control of his vehicle, and stopped on the side of the road. Stunned, he sat motionless, for what seemed a very long time.

Suddenly a woman began to bang on his driver's window. "Hey mister, what's your problem, you could have killed me."

Robert rolled down the window, "Where did you come from, what happened?" he asked

"You drove right through a stop sign, causing me to hit your vehicle." She explained.

"Oh dear God, I'm sorry lady, are you alright?"

"We'll see after I check with My Doctor, my neck's a little stiff."

"We better call 911 and make a report," Robert replied.

"I have no time for that, I'm late for a meeting, my Mercedes is still drivable. Here take my business card."

Robert read the name on the card, Sherry DuPont – Curator. "My wife's name was Sherry, she was French, are you French?"

"My mother was from Paris, but I was born here in Abbotsford. Look, I really need to get on my way and I need your name and address."

"Oh sure, my name is Robert Collins, I was just on my way to my new place at Maple Meadows."

Sherry noticed Roberts vehicle was packed full of boxes, and her eyes came to rest on a framed painting in the back seat.

"Tell me Robert, where did you get that oil painting?"

"Oh those old things, it was my wife's, and I just couldn't part with either of them."

Sherry's eyes widened, "You have two?"

She took her sunglasses off and Robert's stomach did a flip.

He started to see stars and leaned into the back door of his vehicle for support. Her eyes, he only knew of one other person with violet eyes and that was his late wife. Without a word, she turned around and fumbled around in her purse.

"Oh boy.' Robert wondered what the woman was up to. He stared at her back as she talked on her cell phone. She talked in whispered tones and kept glancing at him over her shoulder.

Sherry put her cell phone in her purse. Her heart was racing. She had waited her whole life for this moment. She took a moment to compose herself then turned around and flashed the stranger her most brilliant smile.

"Mr. Collins, I'd like to buy you dinner, and I won't take no for an answer."

Not what he was expecting, well to be honest he didn't know what to expect. This day was a very strange one indeed. He accepted. Something stirred inside him; he had a strange feeling that this woman was somehow connected to his late wife. He had questions of his own for this lady. And, why the interest in the paintings? Robert knew they had some value, but he couldn't guess how much.

She gave him the address where to meet and drove off in her fancy car. Robert stood beside his SUV for a while, trying to fit some of the pieces together. What where the chances of all these similarities between this woman and his wife? He knew from the way she had looked at him, that she thought he was just an old retired fellow with no brains, he decided to play along – for now. He reached in his pocket and pulled out the business card she had given him: Miss Sherry DuPont. He hadn't felt this exhilarated in years. He grinned, he couldn't wait for tonight.

It didn't take him long to settle into his new home. He had little to unpack, the little room filled. His new accommodations were practical, stark and cold. The two paintings brought color and presence, one in his bedroom and one in the sitting room. He considered their hanging for most of the afternoon, hammering small nails into the pristine walls and standing back to judge the placement. He eventually chose a small wall visible from almost every angle for the landscape. The lush greens and warm sepia tones brought life and warmth.

The portrait, he hung on the wall opposite his bed. It would be the last thing to see at night and the first thing he'd see upon waking. The eyes, the familiar violet of his wife's, full of compassion and forgiveness and a small hint of humor, comforted him. He lay on the bed and rested, waiting for the appointed dinner date and considered the odd coincidences.

He'd fallen asleep. The afternoon light was fading when he roused himself and realizing his lateness, rushed to dress. A ten-minute drive brought him to the restaurant's facade. He was an hour late and could see the woman through the large plate glass window, rising from her seat. He rapped with his knuckles on the glass. She looked annoyed, but sat again and re-aligned her face to a tight smile of welcome.

Robert reached her table and extended his hand in a warm greeting. He slipped off his long black coat and flannel scarf. Robert felt the softness of the scarf as he slid it down his neck – Sherry had surprised him with it on Christmas Eve.

He turned now to look at this new woman. Who was she really and why interested in dinner with him? Robert sat down opposite Sherry and ordered a martini when the waitress arrived at their table. He hadn't had a drink since his wife died, but for some reason, he felt a sudden urge to have his favorite drink.

Robert took a deep breath and looked at Sherry. Her beautiful violet eyes glistened. As he looked at her, he felt like he was looking at an angel. Her shoulder-length light brown hair framed her light-olive skin and when she smiled, he became light-headed. Robert's fascination with her did not go unnoticed.

"Robert, why are you looking at me so intently?"

Robert blushed and looked down at his hands. "You remind me of my late wife."

Sherry smiled as she sipped her red wine. "Maybe it's because we share the same name?"

Robert shook his head. "No, it's more than that. You even look just like her!"

Now it was Sherry's turn to blush and she giggled. She rubbed the side of her goblet – a habit she had developed when she was shy or nervous. Then she crossed her arms and leaned towards Robert.

"I don't think I've been clear about my intentions, here, Robert," she said. "I'm really interested in those paintings."

"Oh," said Robert, as he tried to hide his disappointment. Of course, she wanted to meet about the paintings, what was he thinking?

Sherry cleared her throat and continued. "Where did your wife get those?"

"I believe it was from her mother," said Robert. "She took a few classes and painted them. Then Sherry's mom decided to give them to her when she moved into a senior's home."

"The frames?" Sherry's brow wrinkled and one eyebrow rose while the other dropped. Robert felt his heart stop and then start again with a jerk.

"The frames?"

"Yes, the frames. Where did the frames come from?"

"I think she just had them. They were on old paintings."

"What happened to the paintings?"

"I don't know," Robert closed his eyes, as he peeled back the years to his mother-in-law's studio, just a closed in front porch but with good light. He remembered her huge easel; it always held a canvas those last years, and something else. Sure, it came to him suddenly, "she painted over them. She didn't have a lot of money so she painted over old canvases. I remember watching as she hid the horrid old pictures with her own work. Are they valuable? The frames I mean."

"More than you know Robert," and Sherry clapped her hands with a loud crack.

Robert felt something squeeze his upper arm and looked up to see a police officer.

Robert reacted with alarm, as the policeman placed his hand on Robert's shoulder. "Would you please stand sir?" he sternly ordered.

"What's going on?" Robert stood up.

"You're being investigated for possession of stolen art."

"What stolen art?" he glanced at Sherry. The happenings of the day suddenly came into focus. Obviously, she had assumed from the old frames on his pictures that there were valuable stolen paintings being hid under his wife's art work. "That's just crazy, my mother-in-law would have known if there was anything of value in those old paintings. Besides how can you assume they were stolen? You're getting was ahead of yourself here." He give Sherry a "you bitch you," look as he spoke.

"In any event you have to come down to the station with the paintings right now and remain there until some questions are answered."

"Well if I must, I wish to consult with a lawyer before I say anything further."

"That's your right, you can do that at the station."

Robert consulted with his lawyer, who also consulted with the police about the precise nature of the complaint that was filed by Sherry. Sherry had identified herself as the great grand daughter of Otto Gerstenberg of Berlin, he had died in 1935. He had been the owner of a Courbet's painting "The Awakening" which disappeared during the second world war. Sherry claimed the distinctive frame of the picture, of which she had a photograph, matched the frame on Robert's picture.

"You have to let them have the painting examined and perhaps even let them remove the painted over image."

"Do I have a choice?"

"Not really," in the meantime I can get you released on ten thousand dollars bail."

"O.K. Do that, I'm sick of these allegations. Let's go through the whole procedure and get it over with."

Two months later, Robert received a call from his lawyer. "Mr. Collins I have two pieces of good news for you. Firstly that painting was not one done by Courbet, so you are cleared of that complaint."

"Great,what is the other good news?

"There was another valuable1919 painting by Emil Nolde, titled Nadja, under your wife's work."

"Is it worth anything?"

"The art director says it is worth $ 760,000 dollars or more."

"No kidding?"

"Absolutely not! Enjoy your retirement Mr. Collins.

"Thanks, I will. And thank you for your help." His hand was trembling as he replaced the handset.

Robert was stunned. He poured himself a glass of red wine and began reliving the happenings of the past few months; losing his wife Sherry, selling the townhouse, meeting that trouble maker Sherry Dupont, being detained by the police, and finally absolved from any wrong doing." What a wild ride" he said to himself, his hand trembled noticeably as he took a sip of wine.

Looking out the window he saw a car pull into the parking spot next to his. He realized it was Sherry DuPont. Standing up quickly he reached up into the cabinet, then put his hand behind his back and walked towards the door. Upon hearing the knock, he opened the door to a smiling Sherry.

"Welcome Sherry, I'm glad you came. Robert took his hand from behind his back, Sherry's face showed alarm, she started retreating, the color draining from her face. Robert raised his arm. shoulder height, stepping forward. "Would you like a glass of wine?" He stepped back, put the glass down on the table and picked up the wine bottle.

FIRST CLASS VACATION

Vacations cost money, yes they do. Let's explore the true cost of vacations.

A month in Europe can set you back a cool ten grand. If you go to Australia your cost will be twelve thousand plus, Japan will break you financially. A month in Vegas will be only three thousand, however if you gamble you will lose big time. Be sure you buy a bus ticket for home with your last three hundred dollars. If you don't hitch-hiking across the desert will finish you for sure.

Let me give you a surefire way to have a fun filled vacation, and make money as well. Impossible you say, right away you jump to the conclusion that I am talking of becoming a hooker and that you finance your way around the continent with a cell phone and a thousand condoms.

Wrong!

This is perhaps not entirely kosher, but I assure you will have a better time then you first thought. Here is how I did it.

I arranged to rent out my house for three weeks to an out of towner coming for the winter Olympics. That brought in a cool fifteen thousand dollars in cash, even better, no income taxes.

Here is how the rest worked, I'm employed by the International Toilet Paper Company, a company that has a plan that pays my salary while I am on sick leave, again all tax free.

Now all I had to do was get sick, that's the easy part, I phoned my doctor to make an appointment "I have to see him right away." I said in a frantic tone.

"What is the nature of your problem? "cooed the receptionist

"I think there is something wrong with my heart" I whispered weakly into the phone.

The staff at the doctor's office went into a panic, they didn't want me dying in their office, certainly not on their lunch hour! They immediately send an ambulance to my home to transport me to the nearest hospital. So far the plan was working perfectly.

When I saw the medics unloading the gurney in the driveway, I held my breath for three minutes straight. That sent my pulse rate rocketing from 60 beats a minute to 300 ticks, a high enough number to get immediate serious attention.

In no time flat I was on my way to the hospital as fast as the ambulance driver could spin his wheels and blow his siren. They call this "Code Blue "in medical terms. Iin any event I'm taken into the emergency, straight past the thirty people that have been waiting there for the past six hours, my case was a true "emergency "not like those losers lined up in the hall. "If you can't go first class don't go at all,' is my motto.

I had now achieved my basic goal, to be in the hospital, however I needed to make sure they kept me there for at least three weeks. In the emergency bed surrounded by hanging sheets the nurse came in and wanted to take my pulse and listen to my heart -beat. She was extremely attractive, my pulse zoomed up to 360 ticks just like that, no problem. She did her thing, turned pale and requested an I.V. be sent over at once, as well as a blood sucking technician so they can count my white blood cells.

An hour later the tests were back, a doctor waltzed in still wearing his golf shoes, again I lucked out. I knew the guy from the Kinsmen club. He glanced at my chart with a serious frown just like they taught him in medical school "How are you feeling young fella?" he recognized me, even in my sick condition.

I answered "Not bad Doctor, why am I here?" as if I didn't know." I just had a small pain in my chest earlier along with a rapid pulse."

By my suggestion of a chest pain, he went bananas, his malpractice insurance couldn't stand another hit this year. He already had a warning letter from his insurance agent, one more claim and they are done with him, golf buddy or not.

"We will get you into ultra sound right away he promised, your blood work looks good, I don't see a huge problem here at all." he broke eye contact at the last part of that statement, he was lying, the guy was as worried as hell.

Step three, I had to fool the ultra sound technician and her highly computerized machine. This could be a problem, they wheeled me into the semi dark ultra sound room. Again I was in luck,, she was even better looking than the emergency nurse, my heart rate skyrocketed, his time to 360 and stayed there. There was no problem convincing her machine, in half an hour I was on my way up to a hospital bed in the cardiac ward.

As George Bush would say ,"Mission Accomplished"

The time was two o'clock in the afternoon, in two hours I had come a long way. I was getting hungry" Might I be able to have a sandwich?" I asked the ward nurse, "I missed my lunch." I showed her my sincere brown eyes and held one hand over my forehead as though feeling feint.

"Maybe a little chicken soup" I suggested "It might perk me up."

"I'll see what may be left in the kitchen" she smiled, that's her job, to make me comfortable.

"Thank you nurse" I whispered in an ever weakening voice.

In ten minutes I was dining on chicken cattchatori, mashed potatoes with carrots on the side, the dessert was red jello, my favorite. A pot of tea completed the meal.

"We will have to hook you up to a heart monitor machine for seventy two hours" announced the ward nurse. We have to see how your heart functions, you have to write down each activity you do, like walking over to the bathroom, shaving, things like that,. Then our specialist coordinates your activities with the printout on the monitor and we may be able to diagnose your problem."

"What ever it takes to get me out of here, I don't like hospitals." By saying that, I was using reverse phycology, the more I wished to leave the longer they would keep me in the hospital.

The next three days would be critical, not for my health, I knew there was no problem there. I am referring to me failing the heart monitor test. I had come prepared,in my overnight bag I have stashed several Playboy magazines, six boxes of Nicorettes, as well as twenty four "pep up pills" loaded with 100% caffeine. I assure you I would scare the wits out of anyone who read my monitor's print out. Every three hours I chewed up 4 Nicorettes tablets, two pep pills and looked at my magazine for half an hour, until the monitor machine started beeping like crazy It worked beautifully, I was the center of attention.They had to start a second chart by midnight of the second day.

I stayed there for three weeks with all the comforts of home, T.V. to watch, all meals and snacks and a place to sleep that compared with any four star hotel anywhere. Besides that my medical coverage from work paid for a private room I didn't have to put up with some dying, sick old geezer, that might keep me awake or interfere with my TV viewing.

While all this is going on, I was having my pay cheques deposited directly to my bank account, no car expenses, my neighbor was feeding the dog and brought him up to see me every other day. It was heart warming to experience , the dog's love for his master.

After the first week I got day passes of four hours twice a week, so friends came and treated me to dinner out, took me to football games, to the race track, and even to bingo.

By the middle of the third week it was time to be "Cured", I stopped the Nicorettes, was already out of pep pills and give the girlie magazines to the Ladies Auxiliary telling them they had been left behind by some previous over sexed patient. In exchange I got a copy of Popular Mechanics. Two days later my doctor read my chart raised his eyebrows in astonishment and declared me ready to be discharged.

"What was the problem doc?" I asked acting as naive as possible.

"It has us stumped, have you been vacationing out of the country? The tropics perhaps?"

"I can't stand the tropics" I had never been there "I like to take vacations closer to home"

"It may have been some sort of virus, if this occurs again, don't hesitate to come in."

"You never know" I concluded, my mind was already planning next year's vacation.

Now if you have added this all up, I saved ten thousand in vacation costs, received four thousand dollars in sick pay, tax free, the house rent of fifteen thousand. The dog cost me nothing,. On top of that I had winnings from the racetrack and bingo

The only expense was the Nicorettes and pep pills, the magazines don't count as I had them from before. Anyway the total cost was less than two hundred dollars. I was financially better off at the end of three weeks by a cool twenty eight thousand eight hundred dollars.

That, my friend, is how you take a first class vacation.

A WRITER'S LIFE IS NOT EASY

It's not easy being a writer.

You have to get readers to look at your stuff. Then you have to put up with their conclusions like.

"I don't like the beginning," or "I don't like the ending" or "Just what are you trying to say here?" or "People wouldn't really do that, would they?"

So you react and revise the beginning, while you're at it you change the ending. You make the whole thing seem clear and realistic and then it's done. Just like everyone else wanted it to be. Finally in disgust you throw it all in the wastebasket. "Writing stinks."

Then you get another idea. One that will turn you useless life around, but it doesn't. You go through the process again, day after miserable day until the 'writing disease' gets the better of you. Your wife calls 911 and they take you away. The last thing you see are your kids waving goodbye from the living room window, vowing they will never make the mistake of becoming writers.

Sure we get accolades when we write something brilliant, but how often is that? Now don't get me wrong, everything I write is brilliant, in my mind. The problem is other people. They read my well-drafted short story and then they comment, "Not bad." Now that just does not in my opinion do justice to my work, I equate 'not bad' with ' not very good' so what are they telling me? I think that the world is not yet ready for a writer like me. I have to keep my stories from being released to the public until such time as my genius can be appreciated. Like Van Gogh, I will not get recognition in my lifetime.

The real problem I fear is that people are just plain jealous that I write so well and flawlessly. By looking at me you would think, "that joker can hardly spell, much less write, look at his punctuation, his spacing is all wrong. What a sloppy guy. What in the hell is he wasting the few short years he has left, trying to write?"

Now I don't consider my writing a waste. While I am writing, other normal folk are out in the garden getting U V rays by the hour, whereas I am safe inside, my skin protected by sunblock just in case a UV ray comes anywhere near me.

Others go jogging, now there is a waste, what does jogging do? It just makes you want to jog some more, so day after day you jog here, you jog there and pretty soon you are too busy jogging to get down to writing. On occasion however some joggers, while they are recovering from knee and hip operations do begin writing.

Others say they can't write because they experience 'writer's block.' There is no such thing, put it out of your mind completely or you will just scare yourself. Did you ever hear of anyone getting in a car and saying, "I've got 'driver's block' I can't do it". Or a chef who is contemplating scrambling three eggs saying "I have 'scrambler's block, I've never scrambled more that two eggs before, I can't do this." He gives up his chef degree, and goes back to teaching.

Then there is the garage employee who puts air in a tires, gets stressed out and has to take sick leave because he has an ' air pressure block'.

Then as a writer you also have to contend with your spouse's attitude, she of course thinks there are more productive ways to spend your time.

What kind of man are you? "She asks twice week.

"The same one you married 25 years ago." I keep replying

"You didn't tell me you wrote. You kept it well hidden from me, thinking I wouldn't find out didn't you? Well Buster, I have found out, and don't think, for one moment, I'm going to let you keep on writing."

"I am a writer, a very good writer" Hoping it happens some day.

"According to who? Your mother? All she reads is her cookbook by day and her bible by night. That doesn't make her an authority on writing, or you a writer. If you sell anything in your lifetime, I will drop dead from surprise."

"Now that's not a bad idea." I mumbled to myself, but chose instead to answer. "But dear I'm gifted."

"Gifted, a horse's ass is gifted. Furthermore, you can grow flowers with manure. I'm telling you, keep pushing me and I will end up in the loony bin. Maybe you would like to write about that? I'm sure your mother would enjoy reading about how you drove me crazy."

"You're not crazy." I said in a quite tone trying to defuse the situation. "I just need to be inspired."

"Inspired? Well then take those rejection slips out of your wastebasket, sit on them, light them and see if that provides you with inspiration. Maybe you'll get so inspired the lawn will get mowed." She marches out of the room.

Now, am I supposed to be in an upbeat frame of mind, ready to write, after a verbal altercation like that?

Now excuse me, for a few hours. I have to get back to my writing.

THE RIGHT THING TO DO

Mid October, Saturday morning 5 A.M. Princeton, B.C. It is opening season for deer, both bucks and does. A light snowfall covered the landscape, as though protesting the hunt.

Hunters would soon be streaming into the woods, in 4X4 trucks, on trail bikes, and on foot.

Chuck Armstrong looked at the night clock on his nightstand and shook his head, clearing the sleep from his mind "time to get going" he thought. With that he eased his six-foot frame out of bed being careful not to wake his wife Carol, still fast asleep.

Down the hall he quietly walked, to wake his son Corey, this was to be the sixteen year old's first deer hunt. "It's the right thing to do ."Chuck said to himself. Being a seasoned hunter, Chuck wanted his son to experience the thrill of the hunt as Chuck had learned it from his dad.

Corey was still fast asleep. It had taken him several hours to fall asleep, as the excitement of the pending hunt had him imagining various scenes of him drawing a bead on a deer sprinting away out of danger.

"Let's go son, it will be light in an hour, go wash up, I'll fix us some cereal and coffee." Chuck shook Corey's arm.

Corey stumbled half asleep to the washroom, wondering if the whole effort was going to be as wonderful as his dad had described.

He seated himself at the kitchen nook and began picking at his cereal. His dad, already on his third cup of coffee, was all fired up "son, you're going to bag your first ever deer today." Obviously Chuck was more excited than the boy.

After stowing the guns and other related items in the 4X4, they were off. About thirty minutes east of town, they left the main highway and drove for twenty minutes up a logging road that followed Whipsaw Creek. Up they went, into the valley towards the mountains of the creek's headwaters.

Dawn was just breaking as Chuck parked the truck and they quietly exited the vehicle with their gear, being careful not to slam the vehicle doors and alarm any nearby deer.

They slowly worked their was up the gentle moderately pine treed slope toward the top of a ridge. There was a secluded valley on the far side which had excellent cover, browsing areas and a small secondary creek, ideal deer habitat. They kept their eyes peeled on the trail for signs of fresh deer tracks in the light fresh snow.

After about covering half a mile, they came across three sets of tracks crossing the old overgrown logging road they were on. Corey's heart was racing as they began following the tracks, peering ahead into the growing daylight to catch a glimpse of their quarry. The tracks led them down a slope to the small gurgling stream, where the deer had stopped to drink. The tracks continued, as the deer crossed the stream and headed up the ravine to another ridge higher up, where they could bed down for the day.

In the surrounding hills and valleys, rifle shots began to ring out as hunters began the season. Some were single shots, probably experienced hunters having success, others were many shots, as less experienced hunters firing their guns many times, at any animal that dared show its self.

Chuck scanned the far slope with his binoculars. At about three hundred yards he saw three deer winding their way up a well-defined game trail towards denser cover.

"Graduation day Corey" he excitedly whispered. "We will go along our side here and intercept them about a quarter mile along, you should be able to get a fairy decent crack at them from that ridge up ahead."

In six or seven minutes they were in position, another glance with the binoculars spotted the deer about 125 yards away, casually stopping to feed now and again. The doe did most of the foraging, the yearling nibbled at some young willows nearby, while the fawn bounced around, frolicking in the morning sunshine, occasionally pestering his mother for more milk. It was a scene right out of "Bambi", little did the deer know their ideal world was about to be shattered

Ten minutes later the deer were within range about 75 yards away from the hidden hunters.

"Go ahead take your shot, go for a head shot at this range" Chuck whispered to Corey.

Corey hesitated for a moment then raised his rifle, put the cross hairs of the scope on the doe's head, and slowly squeezed the trigger. The bullet slammed home even before the gunshot rang out. The deer jumped high into the air, propelled almost straight up on it's hind leg as the velocity of the bullet drove the animal first up, then down to the ground.

It lay there madly trashing it's feet as though it was running on firm ground. Brain matter and blood was streaming from her head as she half struggled to gain her feet, then fell back gasping her last. Her eyes tried to focus on her family, thinking of their survival, as though telling them to quickly run and take cover. Perhaps sensing her wishes the yearling and the fawn ran about fifty yards into a nearby clump of young pine trees.

The hunters approached the dying deer," finish her off" shouted Chuck "she's still kicking."

"I can't." Remorse had grabbed the youngster by the heart, he was almost crying.

"Stand back out of the way" Chuck curtly ordered, pumping another bullet into the fallen deer.

"You know her hooves could cut you wide open with one slash," warned Chuck, rather needlessly, as the deer was now completely still.

Now the real work for the hunters began. They quickly gutted the deer, stripping out the entrails and lung matter, then wiping the carcass dry with some paper towel. Next they began skinning off the animal's hide, half way through the process they glanced up. There not 25 yards away was the fawn, with big brown eyes intently staring at them, looking, trying to understand what was happening. "Get the hell out of here" Chuck shouted at the fawn, throwing a baseball size rock towards the confuse animal. It moved off a few yards but refused to leave the area. Chuck fired a warning shot above it's head to no avail.

"Lets go!" Chuck was becoming irritated at how things were unfolding. Finishing the skinning, they loaded half a carcass each onto their pack boards and carried their game back the mile or so to their waiting vehicle. The fawn still not wanting to give up followed them at a discreet distance. As the hunters loaded his mother into the back of the 4X4 and drove off, on the wind Cory thought he heard a feint voice in the breeze cry "mamma, where are you mamma.?" Corey was completely disillusioned with the entire outing, it was unlikely that he would ever go hunting again.

Chuck patted Cory on the back. "Good lad you got your first deer."

It had been a successful hunt. It was the right thing to do.

THE HALL OF MIRRORS

I was strolling through the fairgrounds last Saturday afternoon, as I do every year, searching for something "New." The rides were the same; the gambling wheels, darts, ring toss and coin toss games were making me yawn. I was ready to leave. Then I spotted an almost hidden trailer. The sign on it looked enticing,

"Find Yourself." It offered.

I'm always keen on learning more about myself, I approached the attendant. "What's this B.S. about finding yourself?" I inquired.

"B.S.? No sir, not at all, this here is a ,money back ,surefire experience." He answered with a southern drawl.

I was intrigued. "Explain it. How does it work?"

"Sure, first you enter the trailer, it has 10 mirrors. You stop in front of each mirror and push a button. You will be analyzed by a programed chip on the character trait you show. It will grade you against the norm."

"How does the money back part work? What is the gimmick?"

"No gimmick, at all. It's simple. If after going through, you don't agree that you have come out a changed person with a better understanding of yourself, I will gladly refund your $ 15."

"How many customers have you had today?" I asked, hoping to trip him up.

"There have been 49 in the last six hours."

"How many refund requests?" I figured I had him.

"Only one, an elderly lady became ill, and had to be rushed to emergency.

Since I was not an old lady, no risk was involved. I decided to give it a try. Nothing was going to change me afterwards. Tell me how can you change perfect? I'd be entertained and then I would get back my $ 15. I handed him the money.

The attendant gave me a clipboard with an evaluation sheet. "Keep score as you proceed, "he instructed. "You will be shown a number between 1 and 10, 10 is the highest, some are minuses you have to subtract the minus readings, when totaling."

I hurried up the five steps to the doorway and stepped in. The room was dimly lit with darting, laser type lights giving the room an eerie arcade type atmosphere.

I stopped in front of the first mirror, the sign above was marked "Compassion". I pushed the start button. An image appeared on the mirror, not of me, as I thought. It was a crying baby, crying nonstop. I found it most irritating. I pushed the button again, in an attempt to shut the kid up. It screamed even louder. It must be a girl, I thought. I kicked the wall beneath the mirror; the kid went into warp drive. I was on the verge of running out, when the crying stopped. The baby smiled and held up a sign, it read zero. Sheepishly I wrote down zero and proceeded to the next mirror. I vowed I would do better, now that I understood the nature of the test.

"Humor" was next. I wacked the button and faced the mirror. A kid of approximately 5 years old appeared in a raincoat. What's humorous about this? I thought. Just then I felt a warm flow of some dense liquid hitting me on the side of my head, oozing down my neck and in under my shirt. "I've been shot" I screamed! I put a hand up to the warm gooey mess. My fingers found pigeon poop, I had been dumped on from up above. Again I kicked the wall, as I looked back at the mirror. The raincoat kid laughed. Zero again. I moved on.

"Sociable," was third." Now I have them," I whispered to myself "no one is more sociable than I." I would score high on this. I politely pushed the button. The image of a smiling, fortyish, light-

ly clad, blonde appeared, she tossed her long golden locks back behind her left ear and crooned. "My, my, look who we have here." I
felt empowered and moved closer. Being sociable was not going to
be a problem here, my toes were curling. I eased even closer to the
image, pressing discreetly against the glass. At that moment the
image suddenly aged 55 years. I was face to face with a hunched
over, semi toothless, white haired, grinning, granny with sagging
breasts. I jumped back in horror. In a heartbeat all aspects of my
"sociability" disappeared. Granny held up a sign, "2" it read. "Well
2 was better than zero," I recovered and went on.

Number four, "Honest," honest would be a huge problem for
me. I was always straying from one side of honest to the other.
Honest is a word that should never have been borrowed from
the French language. Hesitating, I started the session. A mul-
tiple-choice question popped up "If you found a $100,000 in a
packsack in the park what would you do? 1) Leave it there. 2)
Take it to the administration office. 3) Keep it for yourself. Well
you guessed it, I scored a minus 10.

More scores continued, 0 in brilliant, 0 in fearless, -6 in naive, -7 in gullible, 4 in daring, -9 in stingy, and 0 in talented.
My grand total was a -26 out of a possible +100. Embarrassed,
I shoved the sheet into my jeans and walked over to the attendant. "I want that refund." I could not look directly in his eyes,
as I handed over the clipboard.

"Sure thing buddy," he reached out his hand with the $ 15.
"By the way, I need the score sheet back to show management
why you were dissatisfied."

Red faced, I began reaching for it, then faltered "I was only
kidding about the refund" I said, forcing a feint smile.

He winked "Have a good day then, I'll see you all next year."
He kept the money.

As for me, I had learned something about myself.

I headed for the ice cream stand,my deflated ego needed
soothing.

FOR THE GOOD TIMES

Les entered the Cowichan district hospital and climbed the stairs to the second floor. He had tears in his eyes. Denny his drinking buddy of 35 years was ill. Neither of them could understand how something like that could happen. But it did, he had just seen Denny at two a.m. Les had left him in high spirits, drunk but happy. It was now five p.m., Miller Time. Time to begin their daily beer drinking session.

He entered the dim private room where Denny was ventilating to the hum of several diagnostic machines. With trepidation he approached Denny's bedside, Denny was barely breathing. Les nudged him on the rump." Hi cowboy."

Denny managed to open one eye and seeing Les' worried face, he half smiled and whispered. "Don't look so sad." He smiled again. "I know it's over." He concluded with a small cough that shook the whole bed and rattled the windows.

"You are going to get better, aren't you?" Les sobbed as he sat down and grabbed two cans of beer from his Roy Rodgers knapsack.

"I may or I may not. It's these damned kidneys you know, a genetic flaw no doubt." Denny answered meekly, as Les handed him a beer with a straw in it. Denny took a long sip, sighed and continued. "But life goes on, and this old world will keep on turning." He took another sip and sighed again as the brew hit bottom. "Ah! That's good, I needed that thanks for bringing the beer, and also for coming." He quickly added.

"What are friends for?" Les saw Denny was facing illness like a stand-up man; so he held back his own tears at the thought of losing Denny.

Denny looked at Les philosophically. "Let's just be glad we had some time to spend together." He mustered. "There's no need to watch the bridges that we're burning." They both drank some more beer. Les burst into tears and started sobbing, some of his beer spilled on Denny's sheets and the hospital room floor. Les wiped up the spill with half a box of Kleenex and tossed the beer soaked tissues in the little garbage bag fastened to Denny's bed.

Denny admonished him "Shove those tissues down into the bottom of the bag Les; they look like they've been peed on." Les took a few more tissues and laid them over the soaked ones.

Denny saw his friend was in distress and beckoned him closer with his index finger. "Come here Les my boy, lay your head, upon my pillow, hold your warm and tender body close to mine."

Les hesitated "Look here Denny, I'll hold your hand but you'll have to forget about the tender body part." He took three quick nervous swigs of beer and changed the subject "Do you hear the whisper of the raindrops, blowing soft, against the window?"

"Yes I do" Denny whispered softly, "and make believe you love me, one more time," he continued "for the good times." He pleaded.

Les took a step back, but had to agree "yes we had many good times Denny. I'll always remember you for that and I do love you," he quickly added "I mean love, in the biblical sense of course." Les hadn't seen a Bible since his second and last year of Sunday school.

"Of course Les." Denny sipped some more beer as he tried to calm down Les. "I'll get along; you'll find another, drinking partner I mean." He continued whispering in a gravelly voice "And I'll be here in the hospital if you should find, you ever need me."

Denny interrupted "Don't say a word about tomorrow, or forever, there'll be time enough for sadness when you leave me." Les cracked open two more cans of beer and a package of Frito chips.

"I'll drink to that" whispered Denny as he reached out for the beer.

WEREWOLVES AMONGST US

CHAPTER 1

Was Rolf Unger destined to have close ties to the werewolf culture? Was it because his Hungarian mother gave birth to him on a full moon night? Did his wandering German father, who disappeared two days after conception, pass the werewolf genes over to Rolf? Was this all a bigger plan to infiltrate society by a significant number of these mysterious night hunters?

As Rolf grew, he adapted well to grade school life, keeping mostly to himself. He preferred a few close friends, mostly girls, who would play the games he suggested. They were drawn to his domineering nature and did not question his budding leadership skills.

Once in his teens, his interest in werewolves developed over the years. He read every library book on the subject. Rolf found intriguing the concept of a man transforming at will into a sleek dark silver haired marauding night killer. He memorized the tell-tale characteristics of werewolves when in human form; their musty smell, their bushy eyebrows meeting in the middle of their forehead, having longer than average ring fingers, their prevalence towards early sexual maturity, slowly darkening skin, and a slightly purplish ting in their urine

In fact, he began practicing by imagining taking on the form of a wolf standing at the edge of a clearing surveying the lowlands below. As he closed his eyes and concentrated on his inner being, in effect experiencing the excitement of almost uncontrollable wild animal rage churning up inside him. He lusted to devastate his prey, imagining the attacking rush to overpower his victim, ripping into its' vitals, tasting hot blood and warm flesh as he tore away at the remains of his thrashing dying victim.

A strange calmness overcame him after he had these mental 'test runs.' It was all so right, so natural. He found himself being drawn into repeating the sessions more frequently with increased furor and viciousness.

This was his destiny and he knew it was not only his right but his duty, as well, to develop his extraordinary powers to the fullest.

In college, Rolf chose to study law. His choice was motivated by the thought of ripping into witnesses on the stand. What really appealed to him was the power he felt as he and his classmates performed mock courtroom trials. It reminded him of his werewolf ambitions.

While in college, he dated a first year co-ed, Patricia Dumont. She was a beautiful fiery redhead with an adventurous spirit. The tumultuous affair lasted only a few months. Their passions cooled and they discovered they had similar domineering traits, resulting in countless disagreements verging on violence.

Graduating from college with honors, he applied for and became an assistant crown prosecutor in the Fraser Valley city of Mission The work load was overwhelming at times, but it saw Rolf managing with relish the numerous files ranging from petty theft charges to more serious crimes.

Rolf met and married a gentle submissive nurse practitioner Ely. A year later, they had a son whom they named Lyall at Rolf's insistence. Ely was unaware that in meant 'wolf" in Norse.

Two years later Rolf's career break came when assigned a murder trial. Rolf was shocked when he opened the police file and saw the victim's name. Patricia Dumont, a twenty-five year old legal secretary. It was the very woman that he had been dating in college

After his initial shock, Rolf read the details of the case. Patricia Dumont had been brutally attacked and killed beside a pathway near the stream running through town. The case was unique in that a strange defendant, Gerhard Schroeder, had an even stranger defense claim.

A chill came over Rolf as he continued reading. Schroeder claimed he was a werewolf. Rolf's heartbeat quickened he felt the hair on his head, arms and back rise and tingle. A feeling of anticipation rushed through his body. He shivered with excitement. Feelings much like those from his earlier years' surfaced. Rolf had to steady himself against the desk and force himself to concentrate on the file details.

The defense attorney Mr. AL Solis leaked the werewolf defense to the press. He was proposing to enter on behalf of his client a not guilty plea on the grounds of diminished mental capacity.

"The crazy bastard thinks he's a God damn werewolf!" he reiterated to Rolf as they spoke briefly in the hallway outside the courtroom while waiting for court to convene." How the hell am I going to sell that to a jury?" A questioning look appeared on his face.

Rolf feigned a smile "That's a new one on me Al." He agreed feeling a bit strange, as he was forced to break eye contact with Solis. Regaining his composure, he continued, "Your job is to present the case and convince the jury or judge as the case may be." He offered and then added with a chuckle "Lot's of luck Al. Don't sit too close to your client. He may just take it in his head to attack you. I'll buy you a steak when I win this case."

"Don't talk to me about red meat for the duration of this trial." Al shot back, meaning every word.

Secretly Rolf was looking forward to the ins and outs of this case. It was rekindling his interest in the werewolf culture. He knew he would have to revisit all the past information relating to werewolves, so he could effectively prosecute Schroeder.

As the preliminary hearing began, Judge McTaggart, aware of the public's speculation, smiled briefly as he entered the courtroom and saw the gallery. The room was overflowing with spectators, anticipating something gripping to take place. The judge seated himself, looking at the file before him. He then glanced over at the defendant Schroeder. Turning completely serious the judge again scanned the file as the session commenced.

The clerk began reading the charge of second-degree murder entering it into the court record.

The judge turned addressing the defense table." How does the defendant plead?"

Schroeder stood up, his attorney beside him. "Not guilty." Looking tired and nervous his five foot nine inch frame, skinny build and balding head did not exhibit the appearance of a dangerous person much less a werewolf.

Schroeder could easily have been mistaken for a Sunday morning preacher whose collection plate did not overflow.

The spectators anticipating the not guilty plea exploded, buzzing with whispers. Someone let out a wolf howl. The courtroom gallery exploded with snickers and laughter.

"Order in the court" Judge McTaggart demanded pounding his gavel. "Bailiff please remove that man in the third row." The howler was ejected. The courtroom fell silent.

Al Solis the defense lawyer continued. "Your Honor, we request bail pending the trial date."

Rolf stood up. "The Crown objects to bail, your honor" he pleaded, "the safety of the public should be considered."

Judge McTaggart looked at Solis "Am I correct, you're entering a plea of not guilty by reason of mental defect?"

"Yes, your Honor."

"Then I have no choice. I am remanding the defendant into custody until such time that the Crown has had the defendant examined by a competent psychiatrist. You can make a motion on bail at a later date counselor."

The judge adjourned the session and called on the next defendant charged with violating a restraining order in a family matter. Most of the people in the courtroom quietly filed out. They had their adrenalin fix for the day.

The Schroeder case made headlines in the local paper. Displaying sketches of werewolf likenesses, people were speculating on real or imagined incidents that they thought may have been Schroeder's doing. Schroeder was the topic of conversation in every coffee shop, restaurant, bar and barber shop in the city.

The case rekindled Rolf's previous interest in werewolves. He prepared his case for the prosecution with great care and with much research into werewolf information. Now, with the use of internet information available to him, he was able to get a clear picture of what direction the defense might take.

Rolf knew that by winning this case he would enhance his reputation. The entire lower mainland would be following the news broadcasts. This was a career making case. Figuratively speaking, Rolf could see his stock rising as he turned his sights on the position of Senior Crown Prosecutor.

Three weeks later the medical report from Dr. Morgan was delivered to Rolf's office. The report concluded that the defendant although somewhat delusional was still capable of understanding legal procedures and was fit for trial.

At his next appearance, Gerhard Schroeder was allowed bail in the amount of three hundred thousand dollars, with conditions requiring him to remain within city limits. He was restricted to his residence from five p.m. to six a.m. The trial was starting five months later on January 30, 2010. Fittingly, that date was a full moon night.

Rolf would have ample time to prepare his case against Schroeder. As he prepared he had no doubt that he would be successful in getting a conviction against Schroeder.

CHAPTER 2

January 30th dawned with a few snow flurries dusting the streets of downtown Mission. By ten o'clock there was two inches of slush covering the parking lot. Rolf and his assistant started up the courthouse steps. Rolf had not slept well. Logically, he knew that the defense was grasping at straws with the introduction of an insanity plea, especially one as far fetched as this 'werewolf' theory.

As for himself, he knew the explanation had some value; however it was his duty to prosecute the case on the evidence and let the jury decide on the merits of the defense's claim. Whatever his own opinions were, he had to leave out any personal feelings. In his mind, he was uneasy about the way the case was developing. Maybe his uneasiness was due in part to the fact that on that night, there would be a full moon rising.

That's crazy; Rolf shrugged off the thought as he bounded up the courthouse steps. He mentally decided what type of jurors would be needed. The defense, arguing that a supernatural power had influenced the defendant's actions on the night of the killing would be pursued. Rolf thought about minimizing the effect of those arguments by choosing jurors wisely. Since the case was receiving so much publicity, selecting an unbiased jury would be his first priority.

The court had ordered thirty individuals to attend the jury selection process. As usual, Rolf could see that several already held, in their hands, exemption certificates from doctors or similar documents from employers or others.

The jury selection progressed, excusing four people for medical or planned vacation reasons. That left twenty-six, twelve women and fourteen men. Rolf reasoned that he would select older women. They would be more sympathetic towards the Crown's arguments for conviction then older men. Only, as a last resort would he consider choosing any younger male person.

The first potential juror was a retired man with a degree in forestry. Rolf asked him if he had any opinion on werewolves. The man answered to the effect he had never had occasion to dwell on the probability of werewolf existence. Rolf listed him as acceptable, after questioning him as to his knowledge of the case and his ability to make his decision only on the facts presented. The defense also accepted him.

The answers given by the forester had set the pattern and jury selection proceeded quite quickly. The defense rejected the narrow-minded clergyman for obvious reasons. The accountant for being too logical was promptly also rejected by the defense. The undertaker because he couldn't stop smiling, was excused.

The nurse was, again thought too regimental by the defense. Rolf rejected the philosophy student as too immature. The car salesman was considered as too easy to persuade. Neither party wanted him. The theatre manager possibly biased by werewolf movies, was rejected. The entertainer/singer obviously on some high-powered prescription tranquilizers, was excused.

The twelve people chosen as acceptable consisted of seven women and five men, the two alternates were men. All the jurors were between thirty-five and sixty-five years of age. Rolf was pleased with the jury as selected. He felt they were all mature logical people who would consider the legal points very carefully and not be drawn into the defense's suggestions about werewolves.

The next morning as Rolf entered courtroom seven, the defendant Schroeder and his defense team were already seated. Rolf took a slight step back and gasped when he saw Schroeder. Schroeder was sitting there with a fully-grown black beard streaked with silver, dark black/silver hair down to his shoulders. Dressed in a dark gray suit, red shirt and black tie, he looked like a movie version of a werewolf. The only features missing were pointed ears, fangs and claws.

"The son-of-a-bitch is trying to influence the jury with that appearance. I wonder whose idea triggered this hair growing deception." Rolf began muttering to his assistant. "There is nothing that can be done at this time; we will have to handle the matter through questioning and innuendo as the trial proceeds."

Over in the jury box all the jurors' eyes were riveting on the defendant's appearance. The spectator gallery was buzzing with excited comments. They were here to see a show and the defense was making certain they got one.

Unfazed, Judge McTaggert, came marching in. Court was declared in session. Judge McTaggart began his instructions to the jury, finishing with, "You are hereby instructed that at this time the defendant is presumed innocent, and that the presumption of innocence does not change until the jury begins deliberations. Jurors are not supposed to abandon the presumption of innocence before hearing all of the evidence in the case."

He turned to Rolf "Is the Crown ready to commence?"

"Yes, your Honor."

"Is the defense ready?"

"Yes, your Honor."

Rolf began presenting his opening "Ladies and Gentlemen of the jury we will prove to you that the defendant Gerhard Schroeder did willfully commit the crime of second degree murder in the death of Miss Patricia Dumont. On the night of September 4th, 2009 at approximately 10.30 P.M., the defendant killed, in cold blood, Miss Dumont as she was walking home through Centennial Park in the city of Mission. The prosecution will introduce evidence and witnesses of events that occurred the night of September 4th. The prosecution can place the defendant in the park on that evening, as well as present other evidence to show he committed this murder."

"The defense has entered a plea of not guilty by reason of mental defect. It will be your duty to ascertain the validity of the defendant's claim. You will hear testimony from qualified professionals as to the defendant's mental state and the results of examinations subsequent to his arrest.

The prosecution's witness testimony will prove that Mr. Schroeder knew exactly what he was doing. He carried out a premeditated attack on Miss Dumont, resulting in her death. Thank you Ladies and Gentlemen." Rolf strolled back to the prosecutor's table and flung his file down with resounding finality on his table glancing at the jury as he took his seat.

The Judge addressed the defense table. "Mr. Solis, does the defense wish to make an opening statement?"

"Yes, your Honor" Al Solis took the floor. Looking at the jury for a full three minutes, he turned looking at the defendant Schroeder for another thirty seconds. The jurors were all following his gaze. Then he began: "Ladies and Gentlemen of the jury, we are all saddened by the death of Miss Dumont under very tragic and unusual circumstances." He looked down at the courtroom floor for a moment as if he was either embarrassed by the horrid crime or saying a short prayer for the victim. The jury appearing impacted by the gesture, sat transfixed in their seats.

Solis resumed talking. "The prosecution is required by law to prove that Gerhard Schroeder not only committed his crime but,he did so willfully while fully aware of what he was doing. The prosecution has to prove their case beyond a reasonable doubt".

"The defense will conclusively show that the defendant's state of mind was such that legally he cannot be held criminally responsible for his actions. We will present medical testimony that will clearly show to you that the defendant was incapable of rational behavior on the night of September 4. If there is any doubt in your mind after you have heard all the evidence, our defense arguments and witness' testimony you must find him not guilty. Thank you Ladies and Gentlemen of the jury."

The courtroom fell silent as everyone compared in their minds the two conflicting statements, trying to assess the merits of each.

Judge McTaggert broke the silence "Mr. Unger, is the prosecution ready to call its' first witness?"

"Yes, your Honor, we call Sargent Michael Miller."

Sargent Miller was sworn in Rolf asked his first question. "Sargent Miller, would you give us a brief summary of your police experience."

Looking at the jury Sargent Miller said with pride in his voice "Certainly, I have been with the R.C.M.P. for eighteen years, the last eight years in the serious crimes section." He shifted his eyes back to Rolf, to receive the next question.

"Describe to the jury the events of September 4, 2009 the night you attended to the scene of Miss Dumont's death."

"It was 10.30 P.M. I had just gone off duty and was driving home. I got a report of a woman being attacked in Centennial Park. I was only four blocks from the park so I responded to the call and was the first to arrive at the scene." He hesitated to let the jury digest his words

Rolf coached him "Continue please."

"As I pulled up in the police car, a woman ran over to me. She informed me she was the person who had made the call from the nearby phone booth. She directed me to a heavily treed area about seventy-five yards across the soccer field to the walking path. That path connects the residential area near the playground to the commercial strip mall on the far side of the treed area."

"How large is the treed area separating the two?"

"The grove is about one hundred yards wide. It is a shallow ravine with a small stream down the center, trees and dense brush. There's a small foot bridge over the stream connecting the paths from one side of the ravine to the other." He took a deep breath, gathering his thoughts.

"How is the area lit?"

"There are older single pole street lights ever fifty yards."

"Were the street lights on when you arrived?"

"Yes, the lights must have been on for at least two hours at that time of the year."

"Would you describe what happened next."

Sargent Miller glancing at his notes, continued." Mrs. Simpson, who had reported the disturbance directed me to the pathway as being the source of the distressed woman's screams. My Corporal and another policeman arrived at that moment and we rushed across the playing field to the indicated area." He again glanced at his notes "To the left of the foot bridge a trail goes along the small stream. We found Miss Dumont's body about twenty feet from the bridge.

"Was the victim Miss Dumont, alive at that time?"

"Yes barely, she was attempting to raise her head as we approached. Her head fell back before we got to her. We tried to revive her but she had lost too much blood, there were pools of it all around her head and upper body. We requested an ambulance and waited until it arrived and left with the victim."

Did you continue your investigation at the scene?"

"Yes, we then put in a call for the canine unit, began roping off the scene and searching the area."

"What if anything did you find?"

"The victim's handbag was there about four feet from the body, the identity cards,money and credit cards seemed untouched. It appeared as though she had dropped her handbag out of fright just before she was attacked."

Al Solis sprang to his feet." Objection, speculation, Sargent Millar could not have known the reason for the handbag being dropped."

The judge looked at the jury "Objection sustained. The jury will disregard the last part of Sargent Millers statements. The prosecution can continue."

"Did you see or find any evidence of persons in the area?"

"At that time of day only a few people use the pathway, no we did not see anyone"

"Did the canine unit find anything?"

"The dog picked up a scent of something going down a secondary path along the stream. The ground was so hard there were no visible footprints. Forty yards down the path the scent ended at the edge of the water. The dog could not pick up anything farther down the trail or on either side"

"Was there any evidence of a weapon at the scene?"

"Nothing at all, the wound on the victim's neck and upper body appeared to be made by a jagged instrument. Nothing was found in the searched area to account for the wounds."

"How did you get the information that led to the arrest of the defendant Mr. Schroeder?"

"The next morning after canvassing the area of the residential buildings across the street from the park, we found a witness who saw a male enter the woods at seven thirty p.m. about three hours before the murder. He recognized the man as Mr. Schroeder the chef and butcher from the Gateway Hotel."

Sargent Miller stopped and wet his lips before proceeding. "We attended at the hotel and were told Mr. Schroeder had phoned in sick that morning. We went to his home and after much doorbell ringing Mr. Schroeder came to the door. He opened it, turning away and walking back towards the bedroom. He seemed like a man in a daze."

"Objection to the last word, Sargent Miller is not a medical expert. "AL Solis was trying to minimize the testimony the jury. Was hearing.

I'll allow it on the basis that the jury regards it as Sargent Miller's opinion and not a medical fact." The judge turned to the witness box," continue Sargent."

"We asked Mr. Schroeder to come back to the station and talk to us. He turned to face us. We saw fresh scars on his face from what looked like deep scratches. He said he had a small accident at the hotel kitchen, scratching himself on a towel bar."

"Did he explain how that happened?"

"Yes, he said as he bent down to pick up a hand towel the corner of the towel bar had scrapped against his face when he stood back up."

"Where you able to verify his story?"

"No, we had the towel bar examined by forensics but found no trace of any blood on the towel bar nor on the floor."

"Did you conduct any other tests?"

Yes under the victim's fingernails, we found traces of blood that matched the DNA of the defendant. At that point he was arrested and charged."

"No more questions of this witness."

"Mr. Solis, your witness."

"Sgt. Miller. You say there were no human footprints on the pathway. Did you also look for signs of animal footprints as your canine unit followed the fresh scent?"

The courtroom fell silent knowing what Mr. Solis was leading up to the werewolf angle.

"There were some fresh prints in the mud at the edge of the stream where we lost the trail'"

"Could you describe them?"

"Tracks like a large dog would leave."

"A wolf perhaps?"

"Objection, asking for speculation."

"Withdrawn, I'm finished with this witness." Solis had cleverly planted in the juror's the inference to a dog like animal in the area.

"Step down Sgt. Miller" the Judge nodded to Rolf to call his next witness.

CHAPTER 3

The crown calls "Dr. Nyland."

Rolf began "Dr. Nyland what is your position?"

"I am the city Coroner."

"Did you attend at the hospital where Miss Dumont's was transported and then also at the scene of the attack.

"Yes."

"Describe what you found."

"Miss Dumont was lying in a pool of blood on the operating table. She was dead, had been for perhaps twenty-five minutes, she had suffered massive injuries to her neck and throat, in the form of severe lacerations, her throat had been ripped wide open. Furthermore, there were deep scratches and deep wounds on her hands and arms. I immediately had her transferred to the morgue. The next morning I conducted the autopsy."

"Did you determine what caused the wounds?"

"Not precisely, several things could account for wounds like that."

"Would you expand on that answer? As to the several things."

"An instrument that was dull or jagged, perhaps a serrated knife, or a fork like garden tool, even the claw part of a hammer, anything that would penetrate the skin and then rip through it as it was drawn along."

"Your Honor, I would like to put into evidence the photographs and show them to the jury before we continue?" The photos were marked and the bailiff took them over to the jury box.

The photos showed the exact nature of the deceased's wounds, most jurors took only a quick glance, horrified by the sight, and quickly passed them on. The bailiff then placed them back on the judge's bench.

Rolf continued "Doctor did you find any foreign matter in the wounds or on the victim's body that may have been deposited at the time of the attack?"

"There were six items of foreign matter, soil particles, pine needles, a small piece of food determined to be steak, some animal hair, a sample of blood lifted from the stain on her blouse collar, and skin matter under her finger nails."

"Let's take each of these in turn. The crime scene photographs show the deceased was lying face up, could the dirt from the path been as a result of the struggle."

"Yes, quite likely flew up from the struggle or from the weapon itself if it contacted the ground before the deceased was struck with it. Since no weapon was found I can't say for certain."

"Let's turn to the pine needles, how far was the nearest pine tree?"

"I went back to the scene two days later and measured the distance to the nearest pine tree to be forty-five feet, the height of that nearest tree was approximately thirty feet"

"Could the breeze or wind carry a pine needle that far?"

"No, since they were dried needles, it's more probable they were introduced by some other manner, such as off the murder weapon or off the attacker himself."

"Now, how about the piece of steak? Could you determine where that came from?"

"I am able to say conclusively that it did not come from the decease's stomach contents as the victim was a known vegetarian.

"What conclusions did you reach upon examining the hairs collected at the scene?"

"The hair was consistent with that of a canine hair" possibly originating from the path as people regularly walk their pets along that trail"

"What were your conclusions after testing the blood stains?"

"We did a conclusive match to the blood of the defendant."

"And the skin matter under the victim's finger nails?"

"That too matched the defendant's DNA."

Rolf took a long look at the defense table. Before he spoke" your witness Mr. Solis."

Mr. Solis began "Doctor, could the wounds have been made exclusively by a large animal's fangs and claws?" The jurors sat upright fully alert, backs straight, eyes focused on the Doctor, wanting his reply.

After thinking Dr. Nyland replied "Not exclusively, but yes that could be one of several possibilities." The courtroom began buzzing with whispers. The judge banged his gavel and restored order.

Solis continued "And the scratches and lacerations on the hands and arms, could they be made by an animal attack also?"

"Yes, again one of many possible explanations."

"The animal hair, was it consistent with a wolf hair?"

"Objection, speculation there is no evidence of any wolves present."

"Objection sustained. The jury will disregard that last question"

"Withdrawn," again Solis had further injected his theory into the juror's minds. "The steak sample could it have been dislodged from an animal attacker's jaw as it attacked the victim?"

"In theory yes it is possible."

"Do you have any other explanation Doctor?"

"No, I don't."

"Thank-you, that will be all. I'm finished with this witness." Mr.Solis strolled back to his seat with a more than satisfied look on his face, the corners of his mouth showing signs of a suppressed smile.

CHAPTER 4

January 18th started with bright sunshine. Rolf had used the weekend to prepare for today's testimony by Dr. Morgan the psychiatrist. Rolf felt today would be crucial in how the jury felt about the "diminished capacity" defense.

Dr. Morgan was sworn in. Rolf got down to the psychiatrist's evaluation report relating to his examination of the defendant. "Dr. Morgan, in your report you claim the defendant Mr. Schroeder is "somewhat delusional". Would you elaborate on that?"

"He display's some tendencies towards psychosis."

"Would you expand on that please?."

"Psychosis means an individual's reality testing ability is impaired. At times he is unable to distinguish reality from mistaken belief."

"Is it your opinion that the defendant was aware of what he was doing on the night he killed Miss Dumont?"

"Yes, very much so. A person would have to be much more mentally impaired then the defendant to be unaware of his actions."

"Why so?"

"The defendant has a responsible job as a well trained chef. He maintains a house and family, interacting with neighbors and business contacts. He's fully functional. My opinion is that he knew exactly what he was doing."

Rolf looked at Solis, "Your witness."

Mr. Solis began "Dr. Morgan, you did state he was somewhat delusional. You stated how you arrived at your conclusion that he knew what he was doing on the night of the killing. What was his demeanor when you interviewed Mr. Schroeder?"

"In my view the defendant deliberately acted in a manner that would make me consider him unbalanced."

"What did he do?"

"He wore dark glasses, saying his eyes were light sensitive. He walked or rather he loped as he moved from one side of the room to the other, never sitting or standing still, looking back over his shoulder from time to time."

"Anything else?"

"Yes, he kept licking his scratched forearm."

"Like an animal?"

"Yes, you could describe it in that manner."

"Do you belief in werewolves Dr. Morgan?" Solis stared at the jurors.

"Objection" That question is beyond the expertise of the witness." Rolf wanted to keep such speculation from being too prominent and cloud the facts.

"Objection overruled, we have to deal with this matter at some point. The witness will answer the question."

"No, I do not believe in werewolves." He paused "not for one moment." He reiterated.

"Where did these ideas about the existence of werewolves spring from then?"

"Objection, calls for speculation and the Doctor is not an authority on werewolves."

"Neither am I "answered the judge "I'll rule on the motion after we hear what the Doctor has to say."

"Besides Hollywood movies and European legends, probably from a physical condition called lycanthropy, it's where an individual has an inordinate amount of body hair. The hair is permanent the individual does not actually change into a wolf. There is no evidence such persons have the tendency for committing serious crimes any more frequently than the normal population, it is a genetic anomaly." He added, "It is not a mental disease."

Solis appeared annoyed at the last comment but did not object." No more questions of this witness."

"Redirect you Honor" Rolf smiled and faced the witness Dr. Morgan do you believe in vampires?"

The courtroom exploded into laughter. Rolf had made his point

Mr.Solis, red faced, sprang to his feet "Objection."

"Withdrawn," Rolf closed his file. "The prosecution rests its' case your honor."

"We will reconvene at ten a.m. tomorrow Court is adjourned."

Next day.

"The defense calls Dr. Chase to the stand."

"Dr. Chase, you have also examined the defendant for mental competency? What were your findings?"

"I determined that his psychosis is much more advanced than Dr. Morgan's report stated."

"What did you base that on?"

"Mr. Schroeder exhibits symptoms of an impulse control disorder."

"Explain more fully."

"He has an irresistible impulse to commit acts. Simply put, he can't control his behavior."

"How does that apply here?"

"He killed without premeditation. He was unable to control his actions. It was an act of opportunity. He came upon Miss. Dumont and impulsively, uncontrollably attacked her."

"He acted on instinct?"

"Yes completely."

"Like a wild animal?" Solis smiled slightly as he looked towards the jurors.

"Objection, the Doctor wasn't at the scene at the time the killing occurred."

"Sustained, change your line of questioning Mr. Solis."

"No more questions, your witness."

Rolf rose slowly to his feet "Dr. Chase how long did you spend with the defendant?"

"Two sessions, a total of six hours"

"Your contention is that the defendant was not aware of what he was doing?"

"I didn't say that, he acted on impulse, unable to stop."

"Then he may have known what he was doing, but did it anyway?"

"Yes, you could put it that way. Only he knows what went through his mind at the time of the killing."

"Thank you Doctor." turning to the Judge's bench Rolf said, "I'm finished with this witness."

"The defense calls Mr. Herman Reich."

"Mr. Reich you are the owner of the Gateway Hotel and also Mr. Schroeder's employer are you not?"

"Yes that is correct." The witness sank down in his seat and looked uncomfortable.

"What kind of employee is he? You know, is he a reliable, hard worker?"

"Excellent, he has been with us twelve years."

"During that time did his mental attitude change towards his work?"

"He was temperamental to some extent, but most chefs are." The courtroom was nodding. Many had experienced a chef's temper.

"What was his absenteeism record like?"

"More than the average person, about two days a month"

"Did you prepare a list of those days from your time sheets?"

"Yes, it showed twenty-five days in the past twelve months. I give you a copy of the list at your request."

"You did indeed, do you realize many of the days off coincided with the night of the full moon and the next day?"

"No, I never thought about comparing the dates of his absences to the full moon dates."

"Your Honor, I would like to place this list into evidence as defense exhibit number two."

"So ordered."

"I'm finished with this witness." Solis turned and nodded to Rolf.

Rolf rose, "your honor, I would like to commence my cross examination in the morning. I need time to review the list just introduced into evidence."

"Very well Mr. Unger, we are adjourned until ten a.m. tomorrow."

CHAPTER 5

Rolf had good reason to ask for an adjournment. He looked at his watch. It was two thirty he called Sargent Miller and asked him to wait at the police station until he, Rolf, arrived.

Ten minutes later seated across from Miller, he handed the Sargent a photocopy of the list showing the days Schroeder missed. "Mike, I want you to compare this list of dates with your police records as to unsolved crime reports on or around those dates."

"That could take two days."

"Ok then just check the four months prior to the murder. I need the information by morning."

"Check with me on your way to court counselor."

"I will do that Sargent."

Driving back to his office Rolf had a feeling the defense had deliberately put him on this clue by introducing the absenteeism record of Schroeder coinciding with full moon dates It lend creditability to his defense. Rolf thought, "Did they know I would find something more?" In any event, it had to be checked out. The name of the game, if trials could be referred to as games, was "to uphold justice." Rolf was sworn to do just that.

On January 30[th,] Rolf pulled up at the police station at nine a.m.

Sargent Miller was at his desk. "I've got something that will interest you Rolf." He handed Rolf his report, it read:

June 7, 2009 In the Stave Lake area fifteen minutes west of town, Mr. James, who owned forty acres found a deer in a ravine at the back of his property. It had been killed by what he thought were his neighbor's dog a German Shepard. The deer had it's throat ripped open and was left to bleed out. Only a small portion of the animal had been eaten, the heart. The police investigated the neighbor. They were satisfied that the dog was not responsible, after examining the dog and checking the fencing around the neighbor's house.

They did find paw prints in the dust, prints of a huge animal, leading away from the deer to the nearby woods. They, then led to a secondary road where the tracks ended. From there they saw recent 4x4 tracks leading towards the main highway.

July 7, 2009 In the Silverdale area thirty minutes west of town a rainbow trout fish farm reported a break in into their brood stock holding area. Three dozen five-pound fish had been scooped out of their water-filled pens and scattered on the adjoining walkway all had their heads severed. Again nothing much had been eaten or taken. Entry had been gained through an opening above a water trough that was diverting the stream water into the building. Black silver animal hair had been found in the wood frame of the opening as the animal, thought to be a small black bear had squeezed through. The police assumed the bear had been scared off before it could begin eating.

August 6, 2009 In Deroche, twenty miles east of town three sheep had been savagely killed. The heart of one animal had been ripped out and partially devoured. The owner had had a problem the previous year with rogue dogs. The savagery of that attack was nothing like this recent one. He had managed to shoot and kill one of the rogue dogs in that prior incident. This time he had glimpsed a large dark form disappearing into the darkness, as he ran out upon hearing the remaining sheep making a ruckus in their holding pen. Police could not explain the strange attack.

Rolf went pale as he read the numerous items in the report. This was too much of a coincidence to be random events. There could well be a connection.

January 29, 2010, 9 a.m. Rolf had arranged a meeting with the defense attorney Al Solis.

"Al, how about dealing this case out?"

"Why the sudden turn? You had this case eighty percent in the bag." Solis already knew why.

Rolf showed him the report commenting, "We have one sick puppy here, pardon the pun."

"I see what you mean" Solis winked, happy with this new development." What are you offering?"

"Your client goes to a mental facility for a minimum of five years and stays there until two qualified psychiatrists agree he is no longer a threat. He then goes into a halfway house for a further two years before he gets, paroled for another five years." Rolf did not look happy about the turn of events. He added. "It puts him out of action for twelve years."

"Under the circumstances I tend to agree with you. I will talk to my client. I have to confer with my client. Let's meet in the judge's chambers in twenty minutes?"

"Twenty minutes then?"

In the judge's chambers, they informed Judge McTaggert of the new evidence and the proposed deal.

The judge agreed that it sounded like a workable plan. Mr. Solis had one request. "My client needs today and the weekend with his family to get his affairs in order. He will report to court on Monday morning at 10 a.m."

"Any objection, Mr. Unger?" Rolf considered the request momentarily and agreed. "I have no objection, the request seems reasonable, if the defense doesn't object to the continuation of bail."

"We agree to continue the bail conditions."

"So ordered, Mr. Solis, I will see you and your client in court Monday morning."

CHAPTER 6

It was Friday. Rolf's wife and son had gone to see her parents for a few days. Rolf was to join them the following Tuesday after concluding the Schroeder case. Rolf was being drawn into a mental zone he had not experienced before. Perhaps because of the case he had just spent weeks on, he was mentally prepared for a new challenge. It was 8 p.m. Driving home, he changed into old jeans and sneakers intending to run along Centennial Trail, a loop of trails that went through town into the adjoining forest and back

In fact, the murder of Patricia Dumont by Schroeder had occurred beside this trail. Rolf was out for over a period of three hours during which time he transformed into a sleek, muscular wolf, bounding down one trail and up another, testing the various scents that were suspended in the air hanging there above the pathway.

Gerhard Schroeder had also arrived home, to an empty house on Friday. Fearing for their safety, his wife and his son had left home for the weekend. He saw his opportunity to set out into the stillness of the night woods. It was ten p.m. Gerhard had primal urges pulling at his subconscious. This was his last chance to hunt.

His transformation began as soon as he parked the car and stepped out. He had done this many times. It was faster, easier and more exciting each time.

His eyes turned to a red yellowish green with an inscrutable laser-like stare. The hair on his limbs and the back of his torso filled in at an astounding rate. His animal instincts were getting razor sharp, scents of various animals permeated the surrounding woods. He lay low in the bushes near the trail and site of his last kill. He shivered with anticipation at the next opportunity to sink his fangs and claws into the open throat of his next victim. He had another two hours to go to complete his transformation into a sleek dark haired killing monster. It was the longest hours of his forty five year old life. He knew he was under a time constraint. In three days, he would be incarcerated. Opportunities to kill would be minimal. He had to capitalize on this last opportunity to find prey and satisfy his urges. Time was dragging. From the position of the full moon, he determined it was 11 P.M. He was three-fourths transformed. What was taking so long?

He moved out of hiding. He could no longer stand to remain hidden. Venturing out into the small clearing, the site of his last kill, the scent of Dumont's dried blood in the soil was tantalizing. Pawing at the soil to get an even stronger scent, it was absolutely addictive, never had he been so aroused. Remaining there in plain view, compromising his safety, he began filling his being with the scent and thoughts of the glorious kill.

Rolf was approaching the bridge near where the killing of Patricia Dumont had occurred. He had an unusual sense of destiny as he loped passed the bridge proceeding down the pathway, bounding his way along the stream. He was now a sleek, silent, killing predator, feeling stronger every minute.

He caught a familiar scent. It was unmistakable he had been aware of it for some weeks now. "Schroeder!"

He saw the dark form the animal like figure crouching on all fours sniffing the small area on the edge of the clearing. He picked out Schroeder completely engrossed with the scent in the soil.

This was it; he had to avenge the wrong this killer had been causing. Rolf bound swiftly across the clearing, knocking Schroeder down, over on his back. Leaving Schroeder's underbelly exposed. He was flailing about with his partially transformed limbs, trying to regain his feet, momentarily unable to protect himself. His wild eyes showing terror for perhaps the first time in his life, he saw a huge wolf-form with massive jaws descending down on him from the darkness. Schroeder had met his match. With a half human, half wolf utterance he yelled out, just as Rolf began to tear into him. The yell was to no avail. The jaws of his lunging attacker sunk deep into his throat. His cries were silenced, silenced forever. As the last blood spurted out of his jugular, he recognized the scent of the attacking monster.

"Rolf you bastard, we could have hunted together" was his last thought as life rushed from him.

Rolf felt a powerful surge of satisfaction as he retreated to the safety of the woods. It had been an overpowering experience. Rolf had avenged the murder. He had made his first kill in the name of werewolf justice, and he had tasted human flesh.

CHAPTER 7

Monday, February first. The courtroom was packed as usual. The court was reconvening. Judge McTaggert looking at the clock, turned to address the defense table "where is the defendant Mr. Solis?"

"I was unable to reach him your Honor. When I called his home this morning, Mrs. Schroeder said she had not seen him. She had been away all weekend.

"Why did she not inform the police she would be away?"

"She thought it best to take the kids and go to her mother's for the weekend. Mrs. Schroeder agreed that she would return this morning drop the children off at school and then bring the defendant down to court for ten a.m."

The courtroom door opened and Sargent Miller came in and talked to the court clerk, who in turn approached the judge and whispered a message to him

"Mr. Schroeder has been located in Centennial Park your honor. He is dead of wounds to his throat. He has been dead since Friday night according to the coroner. His half transformed body was found this morning covered with brush and leaves a few feet from the trail along the creek."

The judge addressed the court "I am forced to suspend proceedings until such time as the reported death of Mr. Schroeder is confirmed and fully investigated, is that clear Mr. Unger?"

Rolf answered, "Yes your Honor."

"Court is adjourned." The judge rose and left the courtroom. Pandemonium broke out as the courtroom realized the full impact of the short proceedings. Another murder investigation was triggered by Schroeder's death and speculation was rampant as to what happened.

"His pack turned on him," offered one spectator.

"They don't hunt in packs," replied another. Neither of them knew whether they were right or not.

Rolf began turning and walking towards the door yawning. "Now that this is over, I have to catch up on my sleep," confiding to his assistant. with a satisfied smile. Adding. "It was full moon last night I did not rest well."

"It's this puzzling case." His assistant replied. "I'll be happy when we get back to handling normal cases."

As Rolf pushed open the courtroom door to leave. No one noticed the stage makeup covering the extensive scratching and bruising on the back of both his hands.

Two months later Rolf was riding high on the publicity of the Schroeder case. It had been dismissed once the DNA concluded the half-transformed corpse was Schroeder. He got another particularly horrendous case. A local banker, Justin Stellmack, was charged with hiring a 'hit man' to kill his wife and lover.

The evidence was sketchy. The hit man, "Viny Morelli, who had been captured, implicated Stellmack. Through a mishap in transferring Viny to prison, Viny had been killed in a traffic accident. There was no record of any payments by Stellmack. No other connection could be made between the two. Before the preliminary hearing, the Chief Prosecutor had withdrawn the charges, determining the case was too weak for a conviction. Stellmack was a free man.

This did not sit well with Rolf. Was this a call to dispense more werewolf justice?

He made careful plans. It was two weeks to full moon. In the interim Rolf would study Stellmack's habits, where he went, what he did and how best he could 'be taken care of'. It turned out Stellmack was predictable. Being an expert skier, he went night skiing to Hemlock Valley every Saturday night

The last weekend of the ski season would find the hill sparsely populated. Rolf would ensure be would also be there.

Saturday evening arrived Rolf unloaded his skii's, then purchased for cash a lift ticket for the expert run. He took the chair lift up the mountain. Once at the top he skied over to a utility shed about thirty yards from the lift and went inside. There was a comfortable cot to wait on while his transformation was complete. He read a copy of Field and Stream as he waited.

After two hours, he had transformed to where his animal traits were preventing him from reading. He waited in the low glow of the lift lights that shone through the window. At 11.30, he was ready to kill. He pushed open the shed door and loped down the slope to the first natural rest area 500 yards below the lift. The trail made a sharp turn just beyond the rest area, not visible from the bottom or the top of the lift. It was a perfect ambush location. Rolf waited behind a dense cover of evergreen pines.

Within 20 minutes, Stellmack skied by in his distinctive Canada Olympic ski jacket. Rolf hesitated. Stellmack had a woman companion with him. This needed rethinking. It did not take long. Rolf figured if Stellmack was already seeing another woman she was also more than likely involved in the death of Stellmack's wife. Rolf decided they would both pay with their lives.

He waited for their next run; they would be back just after midnight, perfect. Stellmack was leading, his companion was about fifty feet behind. The trail was narrow. If Rolf took down Stellmack first then the trail would be blocked. When his prey was twenty feet away, Rolf sprang unto the trail. Without being touched, Stellmack fell from sheer fright, landing on his side, his ski poles flailing up over his head. Without hesitation, Rolf pounced, sinking his fangs into Stellmack's throat. Red blood was gushing out of the tear, like water from a broken tap, the blue white snow turned purple-red.

His lady companion screaming in sheer terror turned making an effort to find her way back up the slope. Her cries shattered the midnight stillness as Rolf springing through the air, landed on her back, ripping off her snowsuit with his claws as she fell forward. She did not go down easily. Being in top physical condition, her adrenalin rush give her superhuman strength; however, the weight of Rolf's two hundred pounds was too much for her body to withstand. Collapsing to her knees, Rolf hamstrung her, making it impossible for her to regain her feet. Then he took his time.

She was half-sitting and half-lying on the packed snow, well beyond helpless, blood was streaming from het lower legs. In seconds, her life flashed before her eyes. She was repenting for the wrongs she had committed; she was a willing planning partner in the murder of Betty Stellmack. She had provided the payment to the hit man over a period of twelve months prior to the murderer, monthly cash envelopes of $1000. There were to be twelve more after the murder.

Now facing death she wished it would be rapid. It was not to be.

Snapping his jaws around her right arm, Rolf could feel her bone snap, blood stained her jacket, then the other arm more blood. He worked his fangs up from her lower torso through her intestines and finally her throat. He ripped and clawed until her head was completely severed from her body. The head unceremoniously rolled down the hill to lodge against Stellmack's lifeless body.

It was over. Rolf fed voraciously, first on her heart then Stell-mack's. In the solitude of the mountain moonlight Rolf feasted without interruption, for over an hour.

Romping back to the shed he waited, transforming back to his human form. At three thirty a.m., he skied down the moon lit slope taking a final look at the lifeless victims. He felt jus-tified as he reached his 2003 Silver Honda Accord and drove away. No one else had skied down after the Stellmack couple's run. The lift attendant took the lift down in a direction that made him unaware of the attack on the skiers. They were not found until Sunday morning.

The police closed the entire hill and began their work- up of the scene. Preliminary signs indicated large animal, tracks. The investigators were confused, the prints were certainly not cou-gar tracks, too large for coyote, there were no known wolves in the area. The Sargent in charge scoffed at the idea of a werewolf as suggested by one of the junior policemen who was reminded of the news item relating to the Schroeder trial. "Just do your job as trained investigators and forget that werewolf crap," the Sargent barked at his men.

An intensive investigation turned into a dead end. The case went cold. All skiers using charge cards had been questioned. No one saw or remembered anything suspicious. The lift at-tendants could not recall anything unusual other than the fact that five cars were still in the parking lot when the final staff left. That in its' self was not unusual as quite often the 'après ski' festivities made some drivers reluctant to drive, catching rides with friends, then coming back the next day to recover their cars.

Meanwhile Rolf had been assigned the case. After four months of fruitless investigation by the police, he recommend-ed to his superior that they had no choice but to file it away as a cold case. "Someone did us a favor," he said.

On his own time, he secretly investigated the bank accounts of the female victim. She had been identified as Connie Smith. He saw the $1000 unexplainable monthly cash withdraws. Rolf felt vindicated in all respects pertaining to the Stellmack case.

CHAPTER 8

Unknown to Rolf, the parents of the female victim Connie Smith were influential in the area. They hired "Spike" Clarence Jones a private investigator to look deeper into their daughter's death.

Spike was no slouch; he had been trained in military intelligence. He knew his way around tough cases. He went over the paperwork the family and police give him. He made a note of the $ 1000 cash withdraws. Concluding there had to be a connection between the murder of Mrs. Stellmack and these recent murders, he studied surveillance videos of the night the ski hill murders took place. Although he was unable to identify the person or the license #of the car, he did determine a large male drove off in a silver Honda shortly after 3.30 A.M. on Sunday morning. The police missed that.

He was shocked, he read their report and found that the police looked at the tape until 2 am and stopped., There was no activity after one a.m. Because of the manner and similarities of the murders, he requested a copy of the file on the Dumont and Schroeder case. After some arm twisting, he was given free access to the files

He found that a DNA sample from Schroeder's fingernails had been analyzed but not matched to any known suspect. This was an important clue. He was looking for a male, who driving a silver Honda and who was connected with both cases. He concluded there had to be a connection with a policeman or some courtroom person.

Hanging around the courthouse for three days Spike was watching who was coming and going. At the end of three days, he had identified four possible leads.

Person of interest # 1 was Gordon Poulson driver of the prison transfer vehicle, in which the hit man died. He was a large male thirty-two years of age, he drove a 2003 Silver Honda Accord. His only involvement in the Stellmack case was as a driver of the transfer vehicle.

Person of Interest # 2 was Brenda Williams - a court reporter drove a 1998 Silver Honda Accord. Her involvement was as a court reporter on the Schroeder case. She did not work on the Stellmack case, as there was no trial. Her size also ruled her out.

Person of Interest # 3 was Rolf Unger- Prosecutor, deeply involved in the Schroeder case and the person who worked on all the cases and attempted to get the Stellmack case to trial. He had been over ruled by his boss. He drove a 2003 Silver Honda Accord. His large size fit the figure on the video tape.

Spike picked Unger as the most likely suspect, deciding to investigate Unger first.

The next step Spike decided on was to get a DNA sample from Unger and compare it to the DNA from Schroeder's under nail sample. He went to visit Unger, making an appointment with him on the pretense of discussing his findings so far, not everything of course. "Good afternoon Rolf." How are things?" They had met briefly once before.

"Never better." Rolf appeared relaxed and unwary.

"I need further clarifications some of those cases you allowed me to review."

"Sure, ask away" Rolf began feeling uneasy as he threw his Styrofoam coffee cup into the trash basket. What did this cowboy have that needed further clarification?

"Can I get a photo copy of the list of employees at the ski lodge?" Spike asked in a low normal voice.

"I will be back with it in a minute." Rolf saw no danger to himself in providing such a list.

With Rolf out of the room, Spike went to the wastebasket and retrieved the coffee cup Rolf had just discarded. Spike dumped it in his satchel. From the ashtray, he recovered some chewing gum and wrapped it in Kleenex and pocketed it. Rolf stepped back into the office. "Here you are, these employees were all interviewed."

"I need to see if different questions may trigger new responses." Spike said explaining his request.

"Give me a call if you get something we can use." Rolf extended his hand as a way of showing Spike the meeting was concluded.

"When I get anything tangible I will be back to you. I'm beginning to see a dead end here." He finished with "Mr. Unger, thank you for your time."

"I hope you crack the case." Rolf bluffed he was enjoying the moment, at complete ease.

Spike took the samples to Vancouver to an independent lab, explaining his suspicions to the analyst. The lab was successful in getting a DNA sequence suitable for matching. The police lab after some lobbying by Connie Smith's family provided a copy of their DNA evidence to the independent lab. Spike got a report back a week later. "Got you big fellow" exclaimed Spike to himself, in the car as he inspected the report. The DNA put Rolf at the scene of the Schroeder killing.

Spike had coffee with Rolf's boss William Henderson. After seeing the lab reports and remembering he had seen the covered up bruises and scratches on Rolf's hands after the Schroeder murder. He was convinced, ordering Sargent Miller to put forty-eight hour surveillance on Rolf.

That night was a full moon Rolf did not go home that night.

He worked on files until 8 p.m. then drove the twenty miles to Stave Lake a semi wilderness area with multiple logging roads and black tail deer. He parked his car and walked up the rough overgrown road transforming as he went. Once in full wolf form, he hunted down a black-tail deer and fawn killing the fawn and eating the tender heart as well as some of the sweet flesh. He roamed the backcountry all night enjoying his feeling of power and freedom. Three hours before dawn, he loped down the trail towards his car.

Unknown to Rolf, Sargent Miller and another officer had followed Rolf, and watched him enter the brush. They waited for his return. Four hours later Rolf loped up to the car and lay down beside it waiting for his transformation to occur. He noticed a shift in the breeze and detected human scent. He recognized Sargent Miller's scent. He sprang to his feet and headed for the nearest trees thirty yards away. Too late, the last thing he felt was a searing pain in his left shoulder as a high velocity bullet slammed downward into his shoulder and penetrated his heart. The huge wolf struggled on his side, legs flailing in the air, leaving the muscular body go lifeless on the ground in a pool of dark blood.

Next day the daily news reported the killing of a large wolf near Stave Lake, the first wolf seen in 80 years.

Rolf Unger's wife was notified a few days later that his car had been found at the lake. The presumption, since his clothes were found nearby, was that Rolf had committed suicide by throwing himself off a cliff into 300 feet of cold water. His body was never recovered. The people in the city of Mission were satisfied with the explanations provided

"There is no point in alarming people," stated William Henderson to Sargent Miller the next day at lunch as they placed their order with the waitress at The Steakhouse. "One New York steak please medium."

"Same here, but make mine rarer than rare." Sargent Miller added.

A startled look appeared on Henderson's face as he looked up from the menu, glancing questioningly over his reading glasses at Sargent Miller. *Are there any more werewolves amongst us?* he thought as he surveyed Sargent Miller's grinning face and penetrating eyes?

UNTIL WE MEET AGAIN

CHAPTER 1. FIRST ENCOUNTER

There was electricity in the air the day Howard and Melissa met. Was it an indication of things to come?

Howard, a recently retired office manager, and his partner Shirley had been in town three weeks. They decided to have lunch at the local veteran's club, advertised as a regular Friday event. The tables were occupied, with seats only available on a sharing basis. The volunteer waitress smiled and nodded to a table occupied by two women.

"Good afternoon ladies, my name is Howard and this is Shirley, would you mind if we joined you?"

"Not at all, please have a seat, my name is Sheila, I'm in charge of social events. This is my long time friend Melissa."

Howard extended his hand first to Sheila and then to Melissa. "Pleasure to meet you Shelia, and you as well Melissa." So much for introductions. Psychologists once maintained that you have one minute to make a favorable impression when meeting a new person. Howard had kept this thought with him throughout his adult life, using it many times when meeting new customers and business associates. Why the thought rose again from his subconscious, as he surveyed Melissa across the table, he was unable to say.

As the meal progressed Howard grew more comfortable with the company of their new acquaintances. Sheila was by far the more talkative in fact "a mile a minute" would be an apt description. Melissa more reserved peeking from time to time over her steel rimmed glasses. She had a professional manner about her. She had retired from her many years of work as a conveyance secretary in the steno pool of a large legal firm.

Sheila and Shirley provided eighty five percent of the conversation. Howard and Melissa smiled and nodded almost in unison as the other two rambled on about all the past and upcoming events around town. The topic eventually turned to the next social event Shelia was promoting. "There is a steak night next Saturday with a dance to follow, are you interested?" she looked at Howard.

"Sounds good Sheila, where do I get the tickets?"

"Over at the bar." She waved to get the bartender's attention". "Brian we need two tickets for steak night."

Howard stood up, took the few steps to the bar and paid for both the meal and the tickets.

"Thanks Brian, see you at the dance."

"Take care now" he replied with typical bartender sincerity.

"Thanks for you company Ladies." Howard waved as he and Shirley started to leave. "see you on Saturday."

CHAPTER 2. THINGS DEVELOP

Saturday arrived, the Veteran's Club was a beehive of activity. The dinner had been sold out. The Good Times Band was already setting up their equipment. Howard glanced around and noticed the familiar face of Melissa.

She was by herself at a table for four. She give a quick wave and motioned them over. There was a familiarity developing here that Howard could not explain.

"Just in time." she quipped "How are you two today? "She ran the fingers of one hand through her lower locks.

"Couldn't be better" answered Howard, smiling as they joined her "and you?"

"I'm looking forward to this evening, this band is very good."

"I like your outfit." Shirley complimented Melissa on her Red Blazer, white blouse and dark slacks. To complete the outfit Melissa sported a black pearl-like necklace.

An hour later, with the meal completed and the drinks flowing, the band started up. Howard and Shirley danced to the country favorite "Rambling Rose."

"You're right Melissa this band sounds great" Howard commented as he returned. The band started into their next selection "Amanda." "Would you care to dance?" he suggested to Melissa.

"Love to." They were on the floor dancing. Melissa was an excellent dancer, Howard like most men was a barely passable dancer. However, things went surprisingly well. They danced effortlessly, like a well rehearsed couple.

"Melissa you are a superb dancer"

"As are you." She smiled broadly.

"Only because you make it so effortless"

"Here we are like the Disney chipmunks, giving each other all the credit." They both laughed.

All too soon the music was over. They strolled back toward the table.

"Thank you. That was lovely" Howard said as he showed her to her seat.

"My pleasure Howard."

As the evening passed they had two more dances.

It was the beginning of a special friendship.

CHAPTER 3. THE FRIENDSHIP BLOSSOMS

At future meetings, everything they talk about was magically interesting to the other, they had the same tastes in music, food, politics, social justice. They both liked pets, both were career office workers, you name it, they could have been twins.

They were astounded by how they could almost read each other's thoughts. Neither had experienced such an extraordinary feeling of closeness and kinship. When they met it is like the culmination of a fifty year journey, searching for contentment and happiness.

It was a most unusual relationship, it did not revolve around sexual attraction, as most relationships seem to. Rather it was the meeting of two like spirits coming together, like floating white clouds in the summer sky.

They saw each other at the social functions around town they both attended, admiring each other mostly from a distance or across a table from each other. They were content to be just in the same room together, keeping a discreet separation when dancing together.

All this mutual admiration did not go unnoticed by their partners and other friends in their social group. Eyebrows are raised from time to time. As in all budding relationships there were good natured comments flying back and forth "in the spirit of good fun".

Laughing at small hints that he was "sweet on Melissa", Howard ended any speculation by dismissing them with a comment "Should I dance with someone I don't like? What is the point of that?" That kept the gossip mongers busy.

Howard and Melissa independently came to the conclusion, that if they were at liberty to proceed on the basis of their feelings, it became obvious to each of them that something serious would most certainly develop between them.

Both were presently in committed relationships, which neither of them wanted to or would ever consider ending. This dilemma reinforced and magnified itself as months went by. Something had to give

CHAPTER 4. FUTURE PLANS

Howard came up with an ingenious idea. He suggested that about in 50 years after dying, they reincarnate, then at about age 20 to 25 they find each other again. This way they couldfulfill their desire to be together.

The proposed solution appealed to both. It was the only sensible solution to achieving their togetherness. On the dance floor they quietly explored the possibilities of the idea. For all intents and purposes a person seeing them chatting on the dance floor would think they were merely chatting about the quality and price of produce down at the farm market.

There was much to be considered, many details had to be worked out.

Where would hey meet? Of course they have to pick a site that will be in existence at the date they meet in the future. The obvious place was Niagara Falls. Not only was it a permanent landmark it also has the romantic setting for such a happy reunion. They decide that July 1 would be the most likely time they would be visiting Niagara Falls. They decide to meet there on July 1, 2090 and every July 1 thereafter until they found each other.

How would they remember the chosen site? This question did pose a little more of a problem. They decided that if they reminded themselves of the location on a daily basis while alive, they would be able to retain the information into the next life.

How would they know each other? This is a no-brainer, they would instinctively know each other, as soon as they were within fifty feet of each other. Whether they were man, woman, animal or bird will be of no consequence.

Will their reincarnation be in the same years? It would seem logical that they would be reincarnated within a year or two of each other, so that was not problematic. If they keep going to Niagara Falls every year until successful.

Was any of this plan possible? It may have seemed like an far fetched chance, but to Howard and Melissa it was the only recourse, there was no other acceptable way, it had to be tried.

Was there any chance whatsoever of achieving success? It had the same chance as any other adventure, whether it be mountain climbing, trekking across a continent or embarking on a space mission. A goal could only be achieved by making the attempt.

In short order the inevitable happened, she died, a few days later, aware of her death he died. The plan developed, things happened, as years went by the critical time came to see if they met as planned.

The author has penned four different endings to this story.

ENDING #1 – 79 YEARS LATER.

June 1, 2090. Dawn broke on the Scottish moor about half an hour east of Aberdeen. Twenty two year old Marjorie Nichols roused from her deep sleep, awakening from a most realistic dream. She had dreamed that she was off to Canada to meet her boyfriend at Niagara Falls. The only thing obscured in the dream was her boyfriend's face when he turned to greet her his face was a blank featureless face, no eyes, no hair, no eyelashes, no smile, no features at all. That was when she woke up with a start.

"What the hell was that all about?" she mumbled as she stumbled to the bathroom.

The dream did not fade into her sub-conscious as most dreams do. In fact she remembered she had been looking at the travel ads last night in the "Aberdeen Independent." There was a special tour of Eastern Canada including two days at Niagara Falls, Ontario.

"That's where it came from" she concluded thinking back to that morning's dream.

Throughout that day while working as a nurse at the local long term care facility she kept returning to the dream details.

On her lunch hour she went to the travel agency down the street that had advertised the tour.

"I read about your Canadian Tour."

The travel agent's clerk responded. "That's very popular, in fact we have only five single tickets left for the June 24th to July 15th tour. The next one isn't till the fall for the fall colors in Algonquin Park."

"I do have three weeks of paid vacation for this year, I think I will, yes I will book with you for the Niagara Tour." Marjorie could not remember when she had so decisively made a choice on the spur of the moment. It was as though it was a preordained event, something she had no control over.

The trip was booked and she felt a keen sense of calm satisfaction as she returned to work. Back at work she advised the pay mistress of her holiday plans. "Sadie, I'm off to Canada for three weeks starting June 23."

"When did you decide that?" Sadie asked, she had been after Marjorie to use up her vacation time and just a few days earlier had prompted Marjorie again.

"Let's just say I had a dream" quipped back Marjorie. "Maybe I'll meet Mr. Right at Niagara Falls." She had no idea why she said that. Was she predicting the future?

June 09 2090. Evening was approaching in Victoria as 25 year old Les Schwab was finishing his seaman duties on the HMS Calgary, a Canadian Navy frigate. He had been at sea for seven months and was looking forward to some R & R. He whistled Waltzing Matilda as he briskly walked down the gangplank to shore. The Calgary had just returned from a series of sailings in the south pacific, Australia had been one of their main stops.

Les had arranged a flight home to Ontario to his parent's

farm near Niagara on The Lake. It had been sixteen months since he had been home. He was looking forward to seeing old friends especially his fiancé Linda McPherson, a school teacher in Niagara Elementary. In fact Linda had sent him an email saying she had something of importance to discuss with him on his return.

"Got wedding plans, in mind I bet" thought Les. He felt he was ready to settle down. Maybe a shore job was not such a bad idea.

It was a dull rainy day on June 11, as Les stepped down off the plane and was greeted inside by his father and mother. They were all smiles as he approached him and hugs were exchanged.

It was 2 P.M. Linda was working, Les would see her that evening. He called her cell at 5 P.M. "Hi Honey" he greeted her answering machine "I'll pick you up at 6, we have reservations at the Charles Inn, on Queens street."

In a few minutes he got text message on his cell phone. "Hi Les, I thought I would meet you at the restaurant at 6. I have a PTA meeting at 8, in the other direction" It was short and not so "Sweet" "What's with her "Les thought as he cleared off the cell phone message."

Just after 6 P.M., Les' question was answered soon enough. He saw Linda enter the restaurant and approach his table with a determined look on her face. She was dressed in her work clothes, probably came straight from school. She looked tired and stressed as she give him a peck on the cheek.

"You look worn out honey, is something wrong?" Les stood and placed her chair.

"I haven't slept much in the last few nights." Tears formed in her eyes.

"What is happening?" Les was not a stupid man. He sensed something was troubling Linda.

"I'm sorry Les. I have met someone else, in fact you know him. He's Grant Turner the principal."

"He's married."

"Not any more, his wife caught us. She divorced him three months ago."

"I guess I know what's bothering you, you don't have to say any more. Being a Navy wife is not in your future." Les was disappointed but not overly surprised. Service men have to deal with long absences. Maybe being at sea for months at a time makes a person think of these situations. He rationalized it out. Better now than in a few months, after we were married.

Linda was up on her feet "I'm truly sorry Les" she placed the engagement ring softly on the table. She was gone, out the door, out of his life. The engagement ring was sparkling away unconcerned, as if nothing had happened.

Les spent the next two weeks at the family farm supervising the pickers harvesting the cherry crop. He welcomed the busy workday as it give him time to put aside the pain of the sudden breakup.

At dinner that evening his mother had news for him. "Your cousin Evelyn from Winnipeg will be in town for a few days. She wants to see Niagara falls, would you mind showing her around, you and her were always so close when she lived here."

"I like Evelyn, sure it will be great to see her again."

July 1st was a glorious day, there was abundant sunshine, no wind and the tourist rush was in full swing.

Les and Evelyn had reservations for the 11 A.M. tour boat "Maid of The Mist III." They arrived at the loading dock about twenty minutes early.

While they waited a tour bus pulled up. The sixty occupants poured out in anticipation of seeing the world famous "Falls." Les and Evelyn watched casually as the passengers were greeted by a Niagara Tourist Guide who had their passes already purchased. They lined up to receive their passes.

The fourth occupant caught Les' attention, she was a red haired freckle faced, young lady with hazel eyes. The look on her face indicated that she was sub consciously scanning the surroundings looking for a familiar face.

As she approached, her eyes locked with Les'. As she drew near, she began to smile, just a hint of a smile to start, then she broke out with a full infectious grin.

Les was likewise intrigued with her. He smiled back and made room along the railing so she could get a first hand look at the falls.

"Hi" he said. "Where is your group from?"

"Aberdeen, Scotland and you?"

"Just half an hour up the road. By the way my name is Les and this is my cousin Evelyn"

"Hi. I'm Marjory, pleased to meet you,. You look so familiar have we met before? Have you ever been to Scotland?"

"No, never in Scotland, maybe we met in a previous life." They laughed at the outlandish idea "you never know." He smiled warmly as he accompanied her onto the Maid. "How long are you here for Marjory?"

"Just over two weeks."

"Great, maybe I can show you a few other local sights."

"That would be lovely, thank you." She took his arm firmly as they found their places."

ENDING # 2 – 79 YEARS LATER

June 1, 2090. Dawn broke on the Scottish moor about half an hour east of Aberdeen, 22 year old Marjorie Nichols roused from her sleep, awakening from a most realistic dream. She had dreamed that she was off to Canada to start a new life., She had moved there and was looking for work. At that point she woke up with a start.

"What was that all about?" she mumbled as she stumbled to the bathroom.

The dream did not fade into her subconscious as most dreams to. Throughout that day while working at her job as a nurse at the local long term care facility she kept returning to the dream details. On her lunch hour she went to the travel agency down the street.

As a British subject she could live and work in Canada without restrictions. She decided to take a vacation to Ontario and see the sights as well as inquire about job prospects.

Impulsively she booked a one way flight to Toronto. Back at work she informed her supervisor of her intentions. They agreed she could return any time, if things did not work out in Canada.

In Niagara on the Lake, Les Schwab a Navy seaman from Victoria B.C. was helping his parents on their farm. It was his way of spending his holidays as well as visiting his parents. He was unattached and not yet ready to settle down to married life.

At dinner that evening his mother asked a favor of him "Your uncle William is coming over from Toronto on the long weekend would you take him out for a few hours on July 1.

He likes to see the fireworks at Niagara Falls. He doesn't get out much since he had his accident and is confined to his wheel chair. Too bad he is so young to be only 33 and in that situation."

"Sure mom, no problem I like Willie."

On July 1, Les and Willie were waiting in the gathering evening for the fireworks to start. Willie had his wheel chair and Les had brought two folding chairs so he could put one on either side of Willie so he would not be jostled by the crowd.

As the zero hour approached a young, freckle faced, red haired woman approached them. Once she saw them she instinctively turned their way. When she was within a few feet, her face lit up with a smile. Les saw Willie taking a keen interest in her.

"Do either of you gentlemen have the time ?"she inquired. Hardly a new approach thought Les.

"It's almost 10." Willie replied instantly.

"Thank you, by the way my name is Marjory."

"Hi I'm William, this is my nephew Les. We have an empty seat here, you're welcome to join us."

"Well, yes thank you." She sat on the other side of William.

As the evening progressed, Marjory and William exchanged stories about nursing. She from the practitioners' standpoint and he from the two years he had been confined to a hospital bed. They hit it off like a couple of kids at a birthday party. Before the night was over Willie had invited her to the lodge where he lived for lunch the next day. He was quite certain they needed a nurse for the afternoon shift. Marjory felt a strong desire to apply for the position.

"That sounds like a win, win plan." Les said pensively as he gazed out over the Falls ,pondering his own future.

ENDING # 3 – 82 YEARS LATER

July 1, 2093, the City of Niagara Falls, Canada was bustling with activity. It was the height of the tourist season, it was also Canada day, with the July 4 U.S. Holiday following.

The "Maid of the Mist III "was booked to its' 130 person capacity. In fact the operator of the boat, Captain Stuart, had been making a habit of allowing 50 more passengers than permitted to board the small vessel to help handle the backlog of passengers.

It was 12:45 P.M. the passengers boarded the vessel for the 1 P.M. sailing.

On board was Les Schawb, a young Navy seaman on holidays. He was visiting his parents in Niagara On the Lake. He had decided to take the tour today July 1st. in fact he had taken it every July 1 for the past 3 years. Why he did so was a question he could not answer. He was drawn by some compulsion to make it an annual event.

On board also was Marjorie Nichols a recent arrival from Aberdeen, Scotland deciding to come after she dreamed of visiting Canada. She was looking for employment opportunities in Canada. She was spending the day on this outing to the famous Falls.

The Falls boat tour was to take 45 minutes, people on board waved to those left behind as the vessel pulled out into the Niagara Basin and propelled its self towards the spray and thunderous roar of the falls.

Marjorie worked her way to the front of the boat to get a better view. There on the rail was a space, she moved forward and squeezed into place between a man in his late twenties and a woman in her late fifties.

"Pardon me for pushing in" she apologized as she secured her place. "This is my first tour of the Falls" she added.

"Quite alright" responded Les "You will always remember your first visit" little did he know what was to happen.

The "Maid" was about seventy yards from the closest point to the Falls when a sudden jolt hit the vessel with a tremendous force. A large spruce log had drifted loose from a logging boom on Lake Erie came down the Niagara river, over the falls and slammed broadside into the front side of the "Maid".

People were thrown headlong into the water as the vessel was pushed off balance at a 45 degree angle. Among those thrown overboard were Les and Marjorie. Les being a trained Navy diver kept his wits about him as he surfaced. Being an expert swimmer he was in no danger as he kept his composure. He slipped out of the raincoat, and waited to be rescued. Just a few feet distance Marjorie was in some difficulty. She was laden down by the heavy raincoat supplied by the boat and was barely able to keep her head up. Les swam over lifting her slightly by reaching under her arms. "Just relax, I've got you. You'll be fine." Les assured her. A life buoy landed in the water just to their right, then another. Within a few minutes they were safely in a small rescue boat that had sped over to their area.

"Thank you for your help. I'm not sure I would have made it without you."

"Glad I could help, think nothing of it."

"By the way my name is Marjorie."

"I'm Les "Pleased to meet you Marjorie."

They laughed at their present circumstances, huddled, dripping wet, in the corner of the rescue boat.

Les now knew why he had been coming to the falls year after year. Marjorie now realized that some dreams do come through.

ENDING 4 – 2155- 65 YEARS LATER

It was a crisp October day in Niagara Falls. Les Schawb had just retired from the Canadian Navy and was enjoying his life on the family farm near Niagara On The Lake. His wife of 38 years, Judy, was with him. They decided to visit Legion Branch # 396 on Legion Street for a noon luncheon. They arrived at 12.15 P.M. The Legion was alive with conversation and happy diners.

The last remaining 2 seats were at a table for four already occupied by Brian and Marjorie Nichols, Brian had just retired from the R.C.M Police and they had just recently relocated from Ottawa to Niagara.

Sheldon the Legion manager signed Les and Judy in and escorted them over to meet Brian and Marjorie.

As Les touched Marjorie's hand the most unusual sensation swept through him, as though he had met Marjorie some other time. "Pleased to meet you Marjorie, I expect we will be seeing you here from time to time, after all it's quite a small city."

GIFTED

Being gifted is a curse in many ways.

My gift is being able to predict with some certainty what is about to happen next. I believe the correct word is psychic.

Now I wasn't always psychic. In fact, I remember quite vividly,in grade three it was, I had a run in with Bob the school yard bully. "Do you want to fight?" I naively asked him. He immediately bloodied my nose and the fight was over. I thanked him for letting me live and from then on I was psychic. I ran and told the teacher of the incident and as I predicted Bob the bully got the strap. Luckily, being somewhat slow, he did not figure out who had told on him, and I sure wasn't saying.

As I honed my skill at predicting things, my life got easier. The teacher sent someone outside to the wood shed every day to fetch wood for the school heater. This always happened around 3.30 in the afternoon. Sensing this, I conveniently had to be away in the bathroom at that time. I went through the whole winter of 1949 without pulling the wood detail even once.

I would also predict that if my sister got home from school before me she would be saddled with the task of going to the well for water and other farm chores. I of course purposely took the long slow way home arriving at the predicted supper hour of 6 P.M. in summer and 5 P.M. in winter.

Another prediction I made was that if I chose to sit right up front the teacher would not ask me any questions. She would assume that being up front I would have all the answers ready. I was right she chose to ask the at the back of the class who thought they could hide back there and escape her attention.

When I turned eleven my mother thought it wise to take me over to my cousin's house. He had the mumps and she thought it was better for me to catch the disease at an early age, something to do with my manhood in later years she explained. "You will thank me" she remarked as she ushered me into Len's room. There he was, stretched out on the bed moaning and groaning like a calf with a broken leg and with a swollen neck that could be spotted from several yards away. He couldn't talk so After reading comics in his room for two hours we went home. And sure as hell, I came down with the mumps about eighteen hours later. Mother was overjoyed. I guess her wish for grand children in the future was now assured. I was not as optimistic, however in two weeks I was back in fine form.

A few years later the principle remarked. "There's more than one way to skin a lazy cat."

"Does that mean I have detention?." I remarked.

"You must be psychic?" he offered with a sneer.

"I'm afraid so." I replied and I stayed at my desk while the others hurriedly exited the room lest they also be tagged with a detention.

Now being psychic was very helpful when I began dating. I could tell exactly what the apple of my eye would say when I ask her for a little outing. I quite vividly remember when I asked Joan, that was her name, if she wanted to go down to the lake fishing on Saturday morning at six A.M. She flicked her blond pony tail and politely declined. Her friend Helen who heard all this, jumped in and offered to join me. She often went fishing with her father and enjoyed cutting the heads off the fish as they were caught. What she did not know was that I predicted that Joan would turn me down, after all Joan was the daughter of the owner of the Ford dealership in town and was at a status level somewhat above me. In fact she later became an MLA in the provincial legislature. But I knew Helen liked fishing or more precisely,cutting up fish so I engineered the whole scene to get me an outing with Helen.

As the high school years went by I became known as a very good student, not that I did any heavy studying, I was too lazy for that. What I was good at was taking in the big picture and being able to highlight with a 90% prediction rate what was important in the year's work and what were the most likely areas to be covered in the exams. Then Bingo the things I thought would be in, where there and I slapped the answers down finishing most two hour exams in half the time.

The only thing my method did not work on was that God Damn French course. I took one year of that subject, failed my first term paper and just got by with a 69% on the final exam of the year. And that after putting more time in on French then all the other courses combined. Predicting similar trouble in the next year, I opted for biology, which fit into my way of thinking much better than that lousy French. Course.

Carrying on into adulthood I correctly predicted that I could do better working for myself rather than a larger accounting firm, and I was right.

Then at 27, I predicted that I would be better off married than being single, 38 years later it was confirmed as true.

Being gifted is such a curse. I now predict that you liked some parts of my ramblings. Am I right?

ISAAC WALTON REVISITED

It was a calm evening as my wife Sophie and I arrived at Jackfish Lake in central Saskatchewan, north of North Battleford. We registered for a campsite and parked the trailer. I unloaded my 15 foot canoe. I wanted to get an early start. I had been day-dreaming about fishing this lake ever since leaving Vancouver Island.

Morning dawned, the lake was becoming increasingly turbulent. Just after noon the wind's intensity abated. I could wait no longer. I launched the canoe filled with all my fishing gear and set off. The dock operator's boom box was blasting out Elvis' 'It's Now or Never'.

Close to shore the water was manageable but got increasingly choppier further out onto the lake. The water got darker, meaning I was in at least fifteen feet of water. I prepared to cast out my line intending to troll down the lake with the wind at my back.

A large wave dipped under the boat just as I cast out. The canoe took a dangerous tilt towards the oncoming waves as it slid down into the trough. I over reacted by leaning back and I found myself flying backward out of the craft. The canoe turned completely over with the bottom facing skyward and the gear that did not sink was floating down the lake out of reach.

"Stay with the boat" my mind hollered recalling boating rules. I was in near panic mode, as I had never tested of my life jacket. I thought of my wife and sons and my granddaughters. Was this the beginning of the end of my life? I breathed a sigh of relief, as the vest held me up.

A quick lift and the canoe was upright, but full of water. I looked around for other craft. A young couple was paddling a rubber dingy about a quarter mile upwind from me close to shore. "Help me, Help me" I hollered and frantically waved one arm. Fittingly the boom box was now playing "Who's Sorry Now". There was no response to my calls.

I dog paddled with one arm and towed the craft with the other angling for shore. The waves took me further down the lake. Finally my feet touched bottom and I dragged myself and the canoe up onto the sandy shore.

Hypothermic I walked a quarter mile to the beach area. A kind passerby drove me to my campsite and waiting wife.

LET IT SNOW

Dudley stepped out of his house one February morning, to a yard full of snow, green snow. He glanced left, then right, more green snow.

Malcolm, his neighbor was knee deep in the stuff shoveling nonchalantly.

Dudley hollered over to him. "Hi Mal that was quite a snow-fall we had?"

"Yep" was the reply.

"Does it shovel like regular snow?"

"Mal groaned." Its regular snow alright, my back is broken."

Dudley retreated into his house. He called 911.

A woman answered in a bored voice "911. Is this an emergency call?"

"I called 911" Dudley snapped.

"That doesn't mean you have an emergency." Came back the curt reply.

"Tell me what constitutes an emergency?"

"Sir please! Tell me the nature of your call?"

"It appears to be to learn the definition of an emergency"

"Are you being funny sir?" She growled.

"Is that an emergency?" He questioned.

"No it is not." She barked.

"O.K. then we have established that being funny is not an emergency. Then is it correct to say that being serious would be an emergency?"

There was a pause. The 911 operator finally spoke. "Yes emergencies are serious. It says so right here in the manual. Now I'm asking you again what are you calling about?"

"You wouldn't laugh will you?"

"I'm a 911 operator, I never laugh." She pointed out. "Besides you said it was serious."

"What may be serious to me might seem funny to you. Do you follow me?"

"Tell me what is so serious that I might find funny. I'm curious. Where are you coming from?"

"I'm not coming from anywhere. Are you assuming I'm drunk?"

"Why would I assume that?"

"You inferred I was coming from a bar."

"Are you coming from a bar?"

"No not at all. I'm at home calling 911."

"I'm 911, let's get on with it then, describe your emergency in ten words or less."

"Help" how is that?

"Help is one word. Can you expand on that sir? Help with what?"

"Help, My yard is full of piles and piles of green snow."

"That's twelve words can you rephrase that please."

"I'll try. Now if I leave out help it doesn't sound serious. If I leave out 'my' then you wouldn't know whose yard it is. I can't leave out yard because then you would ask 'My what is full of piles and piles of green snow'. I suppose I could leave out 'full' but that minimizes the amount of snow, doesn't it? I can't leave out green because my call may not qualify as an emergency and I can't leave out snow because you would want to know what green stuff I was calling to report. I'm afraid you will have to accept all twelve words.

"I can't do that."

"Why not?"

"It's against the rules in the manual."

"Can you bend the rules a bit?"

"Bend the rules. Do you know I could lose my job?"

"Is that more important than an emergency?"

"Society can't function without rules. These rules enable me to answer more calls per minute." She had studied her manual.

"We've talked for nine minutes how many calls have you missed." Dudley asked.

"None." She sounded quite certain.

"How many emergency units are out on calls right now?"

"None." She was very certain of that.

"When was your last call besides mine?"

"I've been here almost eleven hours this is my first call."

"There, now can I restate my emergency?"

"Try me; I'll see what I can do."

"O.K. My yard is full of piles and piles of blinking green snow."

"That is now thirteen words you added 'blinking.' "

"Take it out." Dudley offered.

"That still leaves twelve words."

"Take out O.K and snow" That leaves ten words. My yard is full of piles and piles of green."

"Green what."

"Snow"

'We took 'snow' out, remember?"

"You insisted I leave it out."

"No, the choice of which word to leave out was yours."

"Can you send out a unit?"

"We haven't established the nature of the call; I have a blank line here I have to fill it in. I can't leave this blank line on the form."

"Can you spell 'unknown'?"

"Yes, of course I can. I'm a high school graduate. I was fourth in a class of nine"

"Congratulations now simply write unknown on the line about the nature of the call and then quickly dispatch a unit."

"They're on their coffee break can you wait fifteen minutes?"

"I'm not so sure I can."

"I can't interrupt their break, it's a union requirement. Besides by going out on a coffee break they are seen in public, it raises their profile."

If they jumped in their truck and answered my call that would raise their profile too."

"It's not the same."

"Only a woman could say something like that."

She was steaming. "Sir! Have you got something against women?"

"Not until tonight," Dudley assured her, then added" but I'm starting to lean that way."

"Sir, I don't think I care for your attitude."

"Look in your manual; does it say anything about that?"

"I think I'm allowed to end the call if you get rude."

"I apologize" Dudley decided to change his approach; he continued "you sound like a very warm caring person; it can't be easy dealing with people that are under stress.

She calmed down "I do what I can."

"Again the sign of a true professional, how do you do it?"

"I've had fifty years of experience. I'm seventy five you know."
She paused "The boys are back now they're on their way"

"Thank you, you're a dear."

MISUNDERSTOOD OR STUPID

I have always prided myself for being kind and understanding to the women in my life, knowing at all times what to say. After all, my mother was a woman, or so she led me to believe. That's another story for some other day.

Yesterday was my wife Maggie's birthday, or so she claimed.

I know what you're thinking; he doesn't believe or trust anyone, especially women.

Well, I'll tell you, it's not a matter of believing or trusting. Neither do I totally believe that there is a God in Heaven anxiously waiting for little old me.

Again, I digress. I have yet to see Maggie's Birth Certificate up close. Oh she's waved a card in my face a few times, but at six feet away and moving, it was impossible to nail down the day, much less the year. For all I know, it could have been a Kellog's cornflakes box top.

Anyhow, for the purpose of continuing this story, let us say it was her birthday. We got up as usual. I promptly left for the local veteran's club, to celebrate Remembrance Day, from 10 am to 10 pm. I didn't ask Maggie and nor did she offer to join me. I'm pretty good that way. I let her do whatever she wants. I'm not one of those ultra, controlling, freak, mama-loving husbands, who demands a minute-by-minute accounting of his wife's time.

So away I went to do my patriotic duty at the club. When I got home, there she was waiting up for me. From her distraught appearance something was undoubtedly bothering her. Before I could close the door and say hi, she barked. "Do you know what day this is?"

I slammed the door, looked at my watch and replied, "It is 10.15 November the 11th, Remembrance Day, isn't it?" I was quite certain I was right.

"What else falls on November 11th?" Now she was getting seamed and commencing to rub the carpet with her feet.

Then it struck me. "Why, of course it's your birthday, Honey. Happy 70th birthday." I stepped forward offering to give her a big warm birthday hug. That was a mistake.

She held her arm out palm up to stop my advance, Maggie had more to say, much more. "How dare you come waltzing in here and acting like everything is O.K.?"

I had to correct her. "I was staggering, not waltzing, let's keep the facts straight." I grinned. She failed to see the humor.

Stepping toward me, and looking me squarely in the eyes she persisted. "Look buddy."

I usually loved it when she called me buddy. It was apparent this was not going to be one of those times.

She continued. "Don't change the subject. Haven't I been a loyal and kind wife to you for the past umpteen years?"

"Loyal sounds right. Yes, you have been very loyal." How could I argue with that? We hadn't spent a night apart in the 44 years we were together. Maybe that was part of her problem; with me being home every night, even if late on most nights, she had had it too good. That was it I had spoiled her!

She waited for me to answer the second part of her question. "Well, haven't I been kind to you?" she repeated, louder this time.

I stepped back out of reach. "Now, how would you define "kind?" I didn't want to give her the wrong impression by answering incorrectly. I needed to fully understand all aspects of the word 'kind.' I thought, by asking her for a clarification, it would jolt her back to reality and no one, especially me would be hurt.

"Do you really want me to define kind? Well buddy, how about, if I let you live? Is that kind?"

There was some truth in that. By golly, she had me again! I had to agree, "Yes dear that is about as kind as a person can get. I honestly can't think of a single act of kindness that would surpass the act of letting someone live. Yeah, you are a very generous person. I hope, someday, I will be able to measure up and exhibit the character traits you have."

"Cut the crap Ron. What did you get me?" she demanded, thinking she had scored a knockout.

Maggie was always easy to buy for. She returned everything I ever bought her. I thought this time a homemade gift would appeal to her. "Wait here." I said, softly, pointing to the sofa in the living room.

I regularly make up C.D. ' music ' from various artists, to play at the Veterans' Club socials. I hurried into the den, grabbed a couple of C.D.s and dropped them up in a Dollar Store plastic bag. Coming back into the living room, hoping it was not going to be soon renamed the dying room, I handed her the gift. "Here you are, Honey, enjoy them" I sat down beside her and watched her as she took the C.D.s out of the bag. Opening the first one up, she began reading the index of songs on the inside cover.

"The first song says 'Please Release Me', by Humperdinck. What kind of a dumb C.D. present is that?"

"There are many other good cuts on that one, but go ahead, look at the other one, Dear." I knew I was only buying a few seconds of precious time.

She opened the second one. "This one starts with 'Thank God and Greyhound She's Gone'," she screeched as she hurled both C.D.'s my way.

What was all that about? I thought.

As I said, I have always prided myself for being kind and understanding to the women in my life.

WHEN STRANGERS MEET

Gregor read with pride his personal ad in the January 15, 1966 edition of the Vancouver Sun.

High School Graduate, semi professional Protestant male seeks female companion. Object Matrimony. Reply to Box 2222Sun

He was proud of the fact he was able to craft such a cost conscious ad. Proud but not surprised after all he was a Jr. accountant. The words "object matrimony" still irked him not because of what they meant; it was a requirement of all personal ads, however those two words cost him an additional sixty cents.

Oh well! He thought if I get some replies it will be worth the extra money, a man has to be daring on occasions like this.

A week later he had two replies. The one from Wanda sounded interesting. It said "I read your ad. Tell me more. Sincerely Wanda" A woman of few words, he liked that.

He replied "Here is my business card" I will visit you next Sunday at one p.m. Gregor.

At twelve on Sunday Gregor parked his '53 Chevy on the street across from Wanda's house in south Vancouver. He was one hour early, that was his style. While waiting he ate his peanut butter sandwich on brown and finished with a Macintosh apple. He had a sip from his canteen of water and rinsed so his breath wouldn't have that peanut smell.

Every half hour he played the radio to catch the news, and then turned it off to save battery power. He practiced salutations. "Hi there." No that sounded too friendly. "Good afternoon" na, that was too formal! "Hello" no that's a cliché can't use that. "My name is Gregor you must be Wanda?" that was perfect. It would tell her who he was, and it would tell him who she was; saving them a lot of time to do the important stuff.

He saw it was thirty seconds to one; it would take him ten seconds to get out of the car twenty seconds to get to the front door and ring the bell. Perfect.

it with dad." She knew Ernie's pride would not allow him to say no to anything she asked; after all she was his little princess.

"Sure, let's do that" Gregor replied he could see that Ernie would always be a part of Wanda's life and he wondered how long Erie would put up with any man that dared to compete with him for Wanda's affections.

That walk was the start of an enjoyable eight month long friendship.

MEDICAL EMERGENCY #2

I've had two medical emergencies in six months. In the first instance someone was poisoning me, I almost died, but luckily my perfect body fought off the poison. *Talk about bad luck*, I thought as I dialed the BC medical help line.

A nurse with a snappy voice answered. "Medical Emergency Assistance, may I help you?"

"I've suffered a wasp sting." I replied in a weakening voice.

"How many wasps stung you?"

"I didn't think to count, but I think it was one. Yes, it's clearer now, one wasp."

"And why are you calling, are you having an allergic reaction?"

"What's that?"

She paused, I think she suddenly remembered my poisoning emergency. "Are you that crazy guy who thought he was being poisoned." She snapped.

"I resent that word."

"Crazy" she asked

"No, Guy! I'm seventy years old, I should be referred to as that 'crazy gentleman' not that 'crazy guy'."

"I understand, now, lets deal with your present problem."

"Let's, am I in danger of dying here?"

"In all of Canada 6 people died of wasps stings in 2011. That's a miniscule amount."

"This is September how many have died so far this year 2012?"

"It doesn't work that way sir.? Let's get down to the sting and your symptoms. Where did the bite occur?"

"In the den, in front of the computer, I was eating an apple turnover."

"No, sir where on your body were you bitten? Was it in the face or the neck perhaps?"

"Oh, no, I was bitten on the little finger of my left hand."

"How does it feel now, is it swollen?

I put my two little fingers side by side. "Yup the stung finger is 50% larger than the other one."

"That indicates a possible allergic reaction. Do you notice any hives, wheezing, nausea, vomiting, anxiety, chest pain, fainting, speech impairment, or a rash all over?"

"Yes, all of those!" I blurted out, hardly able to speak.

"How could you have all the symptoms? Are you sure?"

"I'm sitting here almost unconscious. I need an anti-venom shot."

"That's for snake bites sir, there are no anti-venom shots for wasp bites. Have you had a tetanus shot in the last 4 years?"

"Yes, I think I have had 4, one every year!"

"That would not be a surprise," she said barely audible.

"Are you mocking me again?"

"Sorry, sir, I got carried away."

"Well, OK now do something before they have to carry me away,"

"Do you have any antihistimes in the house?"

"No, I don't run a met lab here, all I have are two aspirin."

"Why two?"

"My doctor, limits my use to two a day."

"Do you mean you go out and buy 2 aspirin every day."

"I'm very good at it, this is my fifth year, I only missed one day,"

"Let me guess, was it the day you thought you were poisoned?"

"Who told you?

"Now back to your sting. Did you scrap the needle out with the back of a credit card?"

"My credit cards were all taken away last year."

"How about your library card?"

"That's gone too, I had to send it back after they took out a restraining order against me."

"Why would a library get a restraining order against you?

"I stole a book."

"Why not just borrow it, or read it there in the library."

"I was too embarrassed."

"Why?"

"You mentioned it earlier, I had a rash all over my body."

"From a wasp sting?"

"I don't know the cause, I had to give the book back before I got to the rashes section."

"Why didn't you go to the index, look up rashes and turn to that chapter right from the start.?"

"I don't read books that way, once I know the ending, then it's a drag to read any more?"

"But it wasn't a novel, it must have been a medical book?"

"Like I said I like to do things in order. Can you help me here or not?"

"Did you notice a decrease in urination since your sting, and is it darker in color than before?"

"I urinated when the damn thing stung me and not since, and as for the color, is wet pants a color?

"Sir, you are hilarious, but I am busy. Here is what you should do, wash the finger in question, with soap and water, put ice on it for about two hours, take your two aspirin and if you die before morning call me so I can send your brain, to the university, for further study."

And there you have it, No respect. Again I almost died; however with help from the B C Medical care system, and a little luck, I survived.

LIFE HAPPENS

Preacher James launched into his usual 11.30 fist pounding sermon, with an ambiguous opening statement. "Life is what happens to you while you're busy making other plans." He stopped speaking to let the silence magnify his words. He stood stone still, no smile, starrng straight towards the back of the room as if looking for Devine approval. A few people coughed nervously, someone blew their nose, and someone's baby cried, ,presumably wanting an early lunch, his mother discretely obliged

I thought to my self' 'Oh Boy, I give up a day of good pickerel fishing for this! I have to listen to Preacher James tell me how my life may be derailed? After all I was 19, I knew everything.I had a grade 12 diploma. What could this Pontiff tell me? Would it bring tears to my eyes and joy to my heart?

Since I had arrived at Church with my parents, my only option was a 12 mile walk back to the farm. I yawned to ensure Preacher James noted my silent disapproval of his topic. Why couldn't he have preached about the Prodigal Son, now, that was a sermon! It was the typical eat your cake and still have it. That appealed to me. For that, I would have sat upright, listened intently and even clapped when the good-hearted dad hugged his useless wayward son. In fact, I even elbowed my own dad in the ribs during the last prodigal son sermon. He snarled and kicked me in the shin.

Today, I slouched down and toughed it out. The fishing could wait until evening. A nice cool June evening on calm water would erase the guilt the preacher was about to heap on me. I listened to see if he could explain himself.

He continued, "God has a life plan for all of us." Again for shock value, he dummied up for a minute,.

Ya, Ya, Now, there was something I hadn't heard before! I had to challenge that statement. If God had this "Life Plan "for me, why was it not made clear? Give it to me straight from the heart like Bryan Adams sings in his song. Bryan could out preach this guy.

Preacher James must have read my mind, he extended his arm upwards, finger pointing to the heavens. "You may very well ask, why does God not divulge his plan for us?"

I began to clap, but was stilled by dirty glances from the preacher and most everyone else.

He looked at me, "Some of you," he pointed at me "some of you seem to doubt God's wisdom," he give me a threatening look. "You youngsters are impatient. You want things handed to you on a golden tray, it doesn't work that way son." Everyone looked at me. Like good Christians, they were ready to lynch me?

Embarrassed I slouched down even lower on the pew "What's this Golden tray crap about, I thought, ,all I want to do is get out of here and go fishing, It's not like I planned to pounce on Goldilocks or kill the bears.!

He answered his own question. "I'll tell you why. By making us search our minds to determine how best we can serve our fellow man, God allows us do it on our own. That way we can feel good about the life path we have chosen."

"What a bunch of hooey, I thought. Now I knew why I never liked Easter Egg Hunts, when I was a kid. In my mind it would have been more fun to sit down at the breakfast table and have the chocolate eggs right there. It would have saved mom the chore of hiding them behind the outhouse and in the chicken coop, Us kids wouldn't have had to wrack our brains running around in a frenzy. Brother! Complete this sermon before I barf.

"Now I want all here today, to think on this during the week and then tell me next Sunday how this command from God, either changed their life or give them some vision as to their future.

The collection plate got passed and we left for home, $10 poorer, but presumably closer to God and certainly much wiser.

During that night, I thought about that sermon. The congregation pressure was going to focus on me. On the street it 's called "payback time." I asked dad to spare me from farm work for the week so I could "plan my life". What could he say but yes. Actually after ranting for 10 minutes he said OK, well not exactly in those words,. His words were, "get out of here."

"Way to go dad" I barked. "I'm trying to plan my life here!"

Without any further niceties, I borrowed the truck, loaded up the canoe and headed for the lake.

On the first day, nothing much happened other than catching the usual 4 or 5 pickerel. Then around noon of the second day my subconscious took over. I began getting ideas about my future. Was God's plan finally being revealed to me? Halijuillia!

"Well its about time you got around it," I shouted, looking up at the sky. I think He got upset. The sky darkened storm clouds gathered. The lake began churning as wind gusts became more violent. The water turned from blue to pukey gray, even the fish stopped biting. I paddled for the dock, hugging the shoreline to avoid being swamped.

Sunday arrived, the church was nearly empty, most people had elected not to report on their life path. Preacher James didn't seem surprised. He addressed the twelve brave people that did attend. "Did you learn something about yourselves and your life plan?" His demanding eyes rested on me.

Three people held up their hand. Was I one of them? What do you think?

FREE AT LAST

Darkness surrounds me.
Warmness envelopes me.
Pulsing rhythms entertain me.
Undulating motions nauseate me
Day after day, the same routine annoys me
Now a change has come, that interests me
I sense a white light before me
A narrow passage beckons me.
Sliding and twisting, straining muscles propel me
I'm free at last, hi mom, hi dad, it's me.

ODE TO CANADA GEESE

Spring is here with melodies of returning Canadas
Flying with ease through the northern skies

God's way of saying that spring has arrived
Bringing the promise that good things always survive
The Canadas start another season of raising broods
Nothing stops them to their nests they are glued
Soon yellow/grey goslings will be following mamma
Learning all about flora and fauna
In just a few months they are testing feathered wings
Preparing for their first look at southern things
The prairie fall turns colder

Canadas gather as flocks get bigger
Soon they leave us with our winter
While they fly away to climates warmer.
Canadas will be back in six months or less
Promising another year filled with success.
Showing that love and dedication will be rewarded

WHAT IS LIFE?

Is this all there is to life? We look up and ask.
Rocking away, having long completed our last task.
Where did seventy years of dreams disappear?
We sadly ask, as our twilight years draw near.
Were our graduation soliloquies merely quips.
That disappeared, like fog bound ships
We came to earth determined to make our mark.
Now it's time to leave, as our life completes its' arc
What happened to our glorious plans, to set the world afire?
Chased into darkness forever, replaced by some other desire.
If only we could start again and set things straight.
To be unburdened of every devilish trait.
To speak out loud, in western fashion
One more time, with re-found passion
To give us peace of mind, to end the strife.
What is life? Is this all there is to life?

16398561R00089

Made in the USA
Charleston, SC
18 December 2012